WJEC GCSE Maths

Intermediate - GCSE Maths Revision Guides & Practice Papers

We want your feedback!

We know we will never be perfect, but that will not stop us from trying! If you think this book brilliant as is, or feel that it has room for improvement, we want to know. Go to the below website to answer 5 short questions about your experience. It takes most people less than 1 minute to complete, and you will automatically be entered for a **£100 gift card**. Really! No other purchase or action necessary, winners will be selected at random from all entrants.

www.Macklin-Survey.co.uk

Contents

Formulae for the Exam

These formulas will be provided for you on the exam, you do not need to memorize them:

Curved Surface Area of a Cone: πrl

Surface Area of a Sphere: $4\pi r^2$

Volume of a Sphere: $\frac{4}{3}\pi r^3$

Volume of a Cone: $\frac{1}{3}\pi r^2 h$

These formulas will NOT be provided on the exam but you MUST know them and apply them.

Area of a Trapezium: $\frac{1}{2}(a+b)h$

Volume of a Prism: area of cross-section x length

Compound Interest: $\text{Total Accrued} = P\left(1+\frac{r}{100}\right)^n$

Probability:
$P\ (A\ or\ B) = P(A) + P(B) - P\ (A\ and\ B)$
$P\ (A\ and\ B) = P\ (A\ given\ B)\ P(B)$

Quadratic Formula: $x = \dfrac{-b\pm\sqrt{b^2-4ac}}{2a}$

Circumference of a Circle: $2\pi r = \pi d$

Area of a Circle: πr^2

Pythagoras's Theorem: $a^2 + b^2 = c^2$

Trigonometry Formulae: $\sin A = \dfrac{a}{c}$ $\cos A = \dfrac{b}{c}$ $\tan A = \dfrac{a}{b}$

For Triangles ABC where a, b, c, are the sides of the length of sides:

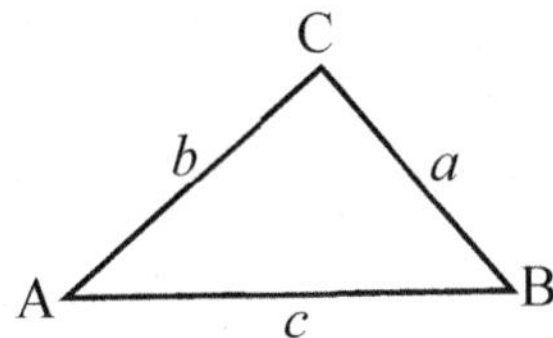

Sine Rule for Triangles: $\dfrac{a}{\sin A} = \dfrac{b}{\sin B} = \dfrac{c}{\sin C}$

Cosine Rule for Triangles: $a^2 = b^2 + c^2 - 2bc\,\cos A$

Area Rule for Triangles: $\dfrac{1}{2}ab\,\sin C$

For full detailed information about the exam, we highly recommend that you visit the official site!

We have an easy URL to type in below to take you right to it:

bit.ly/WJEC_Maths

Section 1: Algebra Concepts

Algebra is a branch of Mathematics with symbols, referred to as variables, and numbers, as well as a system of rules for the manipulation of these. Solving higher-order word problems is a valuable application of the Algebra properties described in this chapter.

<u>Expressions</u>

Algebra uses variables, numbers and operations as the basic parts. Variables are typically represented by letters and may have any number of values in a problem. Usually the variable is the unknown quantity in a problem. All letters can and often are used, but x, y, and z are letters that appear most often in algebra textbooks. In a testing situation, letters other than x, y, and z are often used to mislead test takers. Algebraic expressions are variables and numbers with operations such as addition, subtraction, multiplication and division. The following are all examples of algebraic expressions:

<u>Letters:</u>

| x | y | a |

<u>Product of a Variable and Number:</u>

| $7u$ | $9/2$ | $3.9\,p$ |

<u>Sum of a Variable and Number:</u>

| $s + 5$ | $u+v$ | $2.3+r$ |

<u>Difference of a Variable and Number:</u>

| $z - 3.5$ | $k-n$ | $t - 1.3$ |

<u>Quotient of a Variable and Number</u>

| $m/6$ | $(z/2)$ | $3.9\,/p$ |

<u>Variable or Number with an Exponent:</u>

| c^2 | $b^{0.5}$ | $\sqrt{3}$ |

Finally, the sum, difference, product or quotient of these items are also expressions.

<u>Equations</u>

Equations are defined as algebraic expressions that are set equal to a number, variable or another expression. The simplest identifier of an equation is the equal sign (=). When an equation is written to express a condition or represent a situation for problem solving, the solution is normally completed by manipulating the equation correctly so that a variable or unknown quantity is on one side of the equal sign and the numerical answer(s) are on the other side of the equal sign. Let's review some problem-solving methods in the following examples.

If the simple equation is written in word form, the first step must be to write the equation that represents that written question. The simple problem of ages of individuals is a common example:

Example 1: Jane is 8 years older than Nancy. In 5 years, she will be 27 years old. What is Jane's age now?

The variable J will represent Jane's age and the expression J+5 will represent Jane's age in 5 years. In this example, we read that this expression is equal to a number, in this case 27. Our equation becomes:

$$J+5 = 27$$

In the words of the problem, we have the correct expression set equal to a number. Our basic principle is to perform algebraic operations until the "J" is alone on one side of the equation and the numerical answer is on the other side. This type of solution involves the opposite of the addition (+5) so 5 is subtracted from both sides.

$$\begin{array}{r} J+5 = 27 \\ \underline{-5 \quad -5} \\ J+0 = 22 \end{array}$$

Therefore, the answer says that the variable J, Jane's age, is now 22 years.

If the simple equation involved multiplication, the steps would involve an opposite operation that in this case would be division.

$$\begin{array}{r} 7J = 84 \\ \underline{7J /7 = 84/7} \\ J = 12 \end{array}$$

These examples are typical of "one-step solutions" since a single operation is involved to solve the problem.

Of course, there are multiple step solutions in more involved problems. But the rules are still the same, i.e.

1. Opposite operations are performed to solve
2. The same operations must be performed on both sides of the equation
3. The solution is complete when a variable is on one side and the answers are on the other side

Example 2: Jane is 8 years older than Nancy. In 5 years, she will be twice as old as Nancy. What is Jane's age now?

The first step to solving this type of problem is to identify the variable. In this solution, we will select the variable "J" to represent Jane's age and "N" to represent Nancy's age.

The two equations from the word description, become:

$$J - 8 = N$$

and

$$J + 5 = 2(N+5)$$

Dividing both sides of the second equation by 2 means that it becomes

$$(J+5)/2 = N+5$$

Adding 5 to the original equation we have

$$J - 8 + 5 = N + 5$$

In this method, there are two expressions which contain "J" that are both equal to "N + 5" so therefore, they must be equal to each other. So:

$$J - 3 = (J + 5)/2$$

Multiply both sides by 2 (same operation on both sides) and the equation is:

$$2J - 6 = J + 5$$

Subtract J and add 6 to both sides and the answer becomes:

$$\begin{array}{rcl} 2J - 6 &=& J + 5 \\ -J + 6 && -J + 6 \\ \hline J &=& 11 \end{array}$$

By this solution, the problem is completed and the following statements are clarified:

1. Now, Jane is 11 years old, and Nancy is 3 years old.
2. In 5 years, Jane will be 16 years old, and Nancy will be 8 years old.

We are able to answer the question, "What is Jane's age now?" and all the other ages in the question because of an algebra principle that requires two equations for two unknowns. In the problem, there are two variables (J and N) and two relationships between them (now and 5 years from now). If we are able to formulate two equations with the two unknowns, then algebra principles will allow for the solution of a complex problem.

<u>Quadratic Equations</u>

Quadratic equations are algebraic equations where the largest variable exponent is equal to two. This is often referred to as a "second degree" equation. If there are multiple terms, it can also be referred to as a second degree polynomial, where polynomial indicates that there are multiple terms in the equation. Quadratic equations are valuable in higher-order problem solving situations, with particularly important application in Physics problem solving. Examples are depicted below:

$$7x^2 = 0$$

$$\tfrac{1}{2}(9.8)\,t^2 = 27$$

$$ax^2 + bx + c = 0 \text{ where a, b and c are real numbers}$$

Note that all quadratic equations can be written in the form of the last example because coefficients can be zero and algebra operations can be performed so that the 0 is on the right side of the equation. This last statement is the standard form and is of great importance. **Every** quadratic equation in this form can be solved with the quadratic formula. It is presented here with a qualifying statement. In a timed testing environment, the use of the following formula is typically used when factoring is not feasible, since it a time consuming option. The quadratic formula for equations in the standard form states:

$$x = \frac{-b \pm \sqrt{b^2 - 4ac}}{2a}$$

Due to the complexity of the quadratic formula, it will normally be used when the term

$$(b^2 - 4ac) / (2a) = 0$$

$$(b^2 - 4ac) / (2a) = \text{a perfect square}$$

Since the use of technology is not allowed, any more intricate application of the quadratic formula will be too time consuming to be useful. Note that the operations before the square root sign are both correct. The plus and minus signs indicate that every quadratic equation has the possibility of two answers. It does not say that both answers will be valid to the multiple-choice word problem that is in quadratic form. This is easily explained with a simple statement. Since two negative numbers and two positive numbers multiplied together give a positive answer, any quadratic equation may have two possible correct answers. When answering questions about quadratic equations in multiple-choice problems, that statement should be considered.

FOIL – Polynomial Multiplication

Polynomial multiplication is routinely taught with a method described as FOIL, which stands for First, Outside, Inside and Last. In a binomial multiplication problem, the form will usually look like this, with A, B, C, D whole number coefficients:

$$(Ax + B) \times (Cx + D)$$

The "First" means that Ax and Cx are multiplied together to equal ACx^2
The "Outside" means that Ax and D are multiplied together to equal ADx
The "Inside" means that B and Cx are multiplied together to equal BCx
The "Last" means that B and D are multiplied together to equal BD

The polynomial answer becomes: $ACx^2 + (AD + BC)x + BD$

In testing conditions, this method can be cumbersome, confusing and unreliable because mistakes are too common.

A simplified alternative is called the Box Method, and it is simpler for multiple reasons.

1. There is a box that provides the organization for the multiplication.
2. The box also provides organization for the addition of like terms.
3. This method is expandable for use with longer polynomial multiplication.

To use the Box Method for polynomial multiplication, follow these steps:

1. Create a box that has a row and column for each term in the multiplication problem.
2. Perform the multiplication of each pair of terms.
3. Place the answers in the cells of the box.
4. Add the like terms that are aligned diagonally.
5. Write the polynomial.

The following diagram explains the outcome with the previously noted example:

$$(Ax + B) \times (Cx + D) \text{ becomes:}$$

	Ax	f B
Cx	ACx^2	BCx
D	ADx	BD

The diagonal boxes in the upper right and lower left are always the "like terms" so there are no questions as to which terms must be added. This is true if you have ordered the binomials correctly with the "x term" of the binomials on the left and on top, respectively.

The final outcome is the same as the FOIL answer previously noted:

$$ACx^2 + (AD + BC)x + BD$$

Notice also that the Box Method has the additional benefit of separating the addition and multiplication operations completely.

In a multiple-choice problem such as this, there is a significant benefit in using the box method as a time saving consideration.

Example: $(x + 6)(4x + 8) =$ (choose a correct answer below)

A	$4x^2 + 32x + 48$
B	$4x^2 + 32x + 32$
C	$4x^2 + 32x + 14$
D	$4x^2 + 14x + 48$

The lower right box entry means that the last term in the answer must be 6×8, or 48. So, both answers B and C can be eliminated because the last term is not 48.

The upper right and lower left box entries are added and the middle term must be $24x + 8x = 32x$. So, answer D can be eliminated because the middle term is not 14x.

The correct answer must be A, a choice that can be made logically by looking at the box entries. Eliminating choices is expedited with the Box Method because the box entries can be easily compared to coefficients in the answer choices.

<u>Substitute Variables</u>

Many mathematics applications involve using equations and then substituting variables. This terminology means that the algebra equation will typically have a single variable with all other parameters defined as whole, decimal or fractional numbers. Then to solve a specific problem, the value of the specific variable will be uniquely defined (in some cases, multiple values may be supplied for comparison) and the variables used to determine a problem solution. For example, let's use the equation that was previously discussed, for a car traveling 40 kilometers per hour:

Distance traveled equals 40 kph multiplied by time in hours

Without the words, in strictly algebraic terms:

$$D = 40t \text{ (t in hours)}$$

To find the amount of distance traveled, solve the equation by substituting the value of time that is appropriate for the problem. If the problem stated that the time traveled was two and one-half hours, then the equation would be solved with the following:

$$D = 40 \times 2.5$$

After multiplying, the answer for the distance traveled is 100 kilometers.

In some equations, you may be asked to evaluate an equation that involves a second-degree variable. For example, a word description might read as follows:

Distance traveled is equal to one-half 9.8 m/sec^2 multiplied by the time squared

Again, without words, in strictly algebraic terms the equation would be:

$$D = {}^1\!/_2 \times 9.8 \times t^2$$

Evaluating this equation for a time of 2 seconds becomes:

$$D = {}^1\!/_2 \times 9.8 \times 2^2 = {}^1\!/_2 \times 9.8 \times 4 = 2 \times 9.8 = 19.6 \text{ meters}$$

The answers have distance units that are determined by the units of measure that are given in the word problem.

Kilometers per hour multiplied by hours will provide distances in hours. Meters per second per second will provide distances in meters. The units of time and distance within the problem must be consistent. Substituting variables will be simple if the variables are consistent.

Inequalities – Greater Than and Less Than

Inequalities are an algebra topic that is often misrepresented and taught in a more difficult manner than necessary. When we find solutions to algebra equations there is a single number (or two numbers in the case of a quadratic equation) that represents the set of all numbers that are equal to the algebraic expression on the other side of the equal sign.

Inequalities represent the set of all numbers that are either greater than or less than that specific solution. If the number 3 represents the solution of an algebra equation, then the following number line diagram may help visualize what the inequalities may look like:

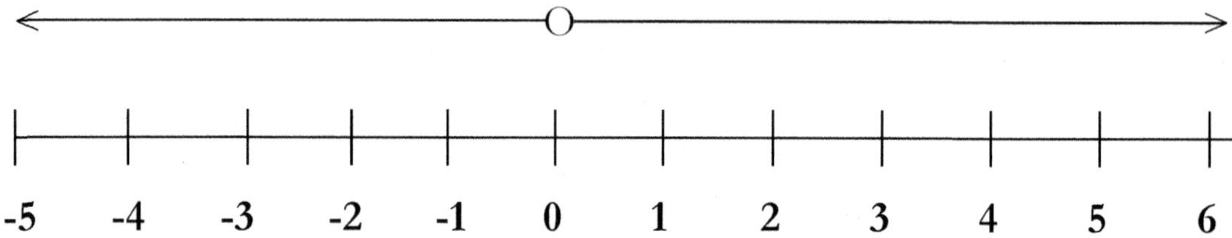

The arrow on the left side of the "o" is the less than inequality, and the arrow on the right side of the "o" is the greater than inequality. Of course, the "o" represents the exact solution of the inequality. This simplicity tells us that the simplest way to solve the inequality is to first solve the equality and then find out which arrow is required. The solution with quadratics will be discussed at the end of this section.

The inequality $7x + 2 > -5$ will be solved by first solving the equality:

$$7x + 2 = -5$$

Following the steps discussed in section 2, the first step is to subtract 2 from both sides and divide both sides by 7. The solution of the equality says:

$$x = -1$$

To see which way the arrow points, we will use the value of $x = 0$ in the inequality to see if it is true. If it is true, then the arrow pointing to the right is correct ($>$), which is what we would expect. If $x = 0$ is not true then the arrow must point the other direction ($<$). The test helps by ensuring that the point at $x = 0$ is or is not in the solution set of the inequality, allowing the correct answer to be chosen. Therefore, substituting $x = 0$ means:

$$7(0) + 2 = 2$$

Since 2 is greater than negative 5 the answer looks like the following diagram:

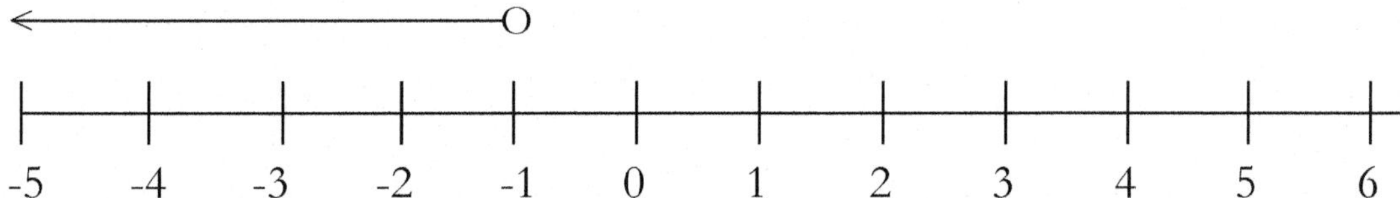

The arrow does not include the point "0" on the number line because the "Zero Test" tells us that that point does not satisfy the inequality. If the "0" is not included then the arrow must point to the left of the point at -1, which was the answer to the equality. If our test showed that the "0" satisfied the equality, then the arrow would have pointed to the right. For this reason, both "Greater Than" and "Less Than" are addressed in this section. They are determined the same way, specifically:

First, find the solution to the **equality**.

Second, test to see if x = 0 is true for the **inequality**.

If the test is true, the solution must include the point x = 0.
If the test is not true, the inequality goes the opposite direction.

There may be the question as to why the value of x = 0 is chosen for the test. Simply, it represents the simplest solution for evaluating algebra equations with variables. Any term which has an "x" (or x^2 or higher order) simply disappears when x = 0, leaving only the constant numerical terms.

If there is a need to solve an inequality where the equality solution is x = 0, then the inequality test can be performed with x = 1. The test is **almost** as simple as the zero test, and it applies if the equality solution is 0. The same logical decision process used for the zero test also applies here.

Section 2: Arithmetic

Many math exams will test your memory of basic math definitions, vocabulary, and formulas that have become so distant that the questions on this type of exam may feel unfair. You likely don't refer to quotients and integers in your day-to-day life, so testing your recall of high school math class vocabulary and concepts doesn't exactly feel like a valid way to gauge your mathematical reasoning abilities.

In this section, it's best for you to begin with a refresher list so that you can master basic math terminology quickly.

Integer: Any whole number, i.e. any number that doesn't include a non-zero fraction or decimal. Negative whole numbers, positive whole numbers, and 0 are all integers. 3.1415 is not an integer. ½ is not an integer. -47, -12, 0, 15, and 1,415,000 are all integers.

Positive and Negative Numbers: A positive number is any number greater than zero. A negative number is any number less than zero. Zero is neither positive nor negative. Adding a negative number is the same as subtracting the positive value of that number. Subtracting a negative number is the same as adding a positive number.

Even and Odd Numbers: An even number is any number that can be evenly divided by 2, with no remainder left over. -4, 2, 6, 24, and 114 are all even numbers. An odd number has a remainder of 1 when it is divided by 2. -19, 1, 3, 5, 17, and 451 are all odd numbers. Another way to think about even/odd is that even numbers are all integers that are multiples of two, and odd numbers are any integers that are *not* multiples of two.

Factors and Multiples: The factors of a number (or a polynomial) are all of the numbers that can be multiplied together to get the first number. For example, the following pairs of numbers can be multiplied to get 16: 1×16, 2×8 and 4×4. Therefore, the factors of 16 are 1, 2, 4, 8, and 16. Note: a polynomial is an expression that can have constants, variables and exponents, and that can be combined using addition, subtraction, multiplication and division.

Prime number: An integer that only has two factors: 1 and itself. There are two things to remember: (1) out of all of the infinite integers in existence, there is only one prime number that is even, and that is the number 2 — that's it, and (2) you can handle almost any prime number question on the test by memorizing all of the primes between 0 and

100. This is not required, but you will save time and mental anguish if you do this. Here they are:

2, 3, 5, 7, 11, 13, 17, 19, 23, 29, 31, 37, 41, 43, 47, 53, 59, 61, 67, 71, 73, 79, 83, 87, 89

Prime Factorization: The prime numbers you have to multiply to get a number. Take the number 24. First, you should find the factors of 24: 1, 2, 3, 4, 6, 8, and 12. Then, you need to pull out all the numbers that are not prime: 1, 4, 6, 8, and 12. What's left? 2 and 3 are the prime factors of 24! Now, that's a simple example, but the concept remains the same, no matter how large the number. When in doubt, start working from the number 2 (the smallest prime), which will be a factor of any number that ends with an even number. Be on the lookout for sneaky questions. For example, if the exam asks you for the prime factors of the number 31, for instance, recall that 31 is a prime number (but 1 is not!) so the only prime factor it can possibly have is itself — 31. The same goes for all prime numbers.

Sum: Add — the number you get when you add one number to another number.

Difference: Subtract — the number you get when you subtract one number from another number.

Product: Multiply — the number you get when you multiply one number by another number.

Quotient: Divide — the number you get when you divide one number by another number.

Expressions

An expression is made up of terms that are numbers, variables, and operators which are added together. If that sounds complicated, expressions are simply made up of the basic symbols used to create everything from first-grade addition problems to formulas and equations used in calculus. The individual terms of the expression are added to each other as individual parts of the expression. Remember that expressions may stand for single numbers, and use basic operators like $\times$ and $\div$. However, a single expression does not suggest a comparison (or equivalency). But an equation does and can be represented by a simple expression equal to a number. For example, $3 + 2 = 1 + 4$ is an equation, because it uses the equal sign. So, think of $3 + 2$ and $1 + 4$ as building blocks — they are the expressions that, when joined together by an equal sign, make up an equation. Another way to think of an expression is that it is essentially a math metaphor used to represent another number.

Order of Operations

An operation is what a symbol does. The operation of a + sign, for instance, is to add. That's easy enough, but what happens if you run into a problem like this?

$$44 - (3^2 \times 2 + 6) = \text{?}$$

You have to solve this equation by simplifying it, but if you do it in the wrong order, you will get the wrong answer. This is an incredibly important concept. This is where the Order of Operations comes in — here's what you have to remember.

1. Parentheses
2. Exponents
3. Multiplication and division (from left to right)
4. Addition and subtraction (from left to right)

You must do these operations in order, starting with parentheses first and addition/subtraction last, in order to get the correct answer.

$$44 - (3^2 \times 2 + 6) = \text{?}$$

Start by focusing on the expression in parentheses first. Inside the parentheses, you will find an exponent, so do that first so that you can do the operation within the parentheses:

$$3^2 = 3 \times 3 = 9$$

then the expression becomes $(9 \times 2 + 6)$

To complete the operation within the paragraph, you need to remember to do the multiplication operation first:

$$9 \times 2 = 18$$

$$(18 + 6) = 24$$

You don't need the parentheses anymore because there are no operations left to complete inside of them. Now the problem looks like this:

$$44 - 24 = ?$$

$$20 = ?$$

You can use the phrase, **P**lease **E**xcuse **M**y **D**ear **A**unt **S**ally as a useful mnemonic. It has the same first letters as parentheses, exponents, multiplication, division, addition, subtraction.

However, the most common mistake involving the order of operations is the following: doing division after multiplication and subtraction after addition, which results in the wrong answer. You have to do multiplication and division as you encounter it from left to right, and the same goes for addition and subtraction. Remember to do what is inside parentheses first, and that might require you to do exponents, multiplication/division, and addition/subtraction first.

Here's another example of this concept:

$$(4^2 + 5^3 - 120) \times 3 = ?$$

$$4^2 = 4 \times 4 = 16$$

$$5^3 = 5 \times 5 \times 5 = 125$$

$$(16 + 125 - 120) \times 3 = ?$$

$$21 \times 3 = ?$$

$$63 = ?$$

If you didn't understand this example, you should go back and review the Order of Operations again.

Occasionally, you may encounter an equation that uses brackets. You should think of brackets as super parentheses, i.e. it's at the top of the list, and so you do that first, before anything else.

Equations

Equations relate expressions to one another with an equal sign. In algebra, they can get pretty complicated, but in arithmetic, equations often center around finding the equivalent of a single expression. For instance,

$$3 + 2 = 5$$

It may seem pretty simple to say $3 + 2$ expresses 5 because they have a clear and simple relationship — they are equal. Other kinds of equations, i.e. relationships, include symbols like $>$ (greater than) and $<$ (lesser than), which can join two expressions together. These are often called inequalities since they are not equal. The greater than or less than relation is a sign of inequality.

Remember that equations can be rearranged by doing the same operations to each side of the equivalency. Here's an example of subtracting 6 from both sides of the equation:

$$34 - 23 = 6 + ?$$

$$34 - 23 - 6 = 6 + ? - 6$$

The number 6 subtracted on both sides of the equation cancel each other out. The equality of the relation remains unaffected.

$$11 - 6 = ?$$

$$5 = ?$$

Greatest Common Factor
=====================

Sometimes the term Greatest Common Factor is called the Greatest Common Divisor, but either way, the concept is the same - it's the largest factor that two (or more) numbers share.

To use this concept, you should first work out all of the factors for each number and then find the largest factor they have in common. For example, find the Greatest Common Factor of 18 and 30:

The factors of 18 are: 1, 2, 3, 6, 9 and 18
The factors of 30 are: 1, 2, 3, 5, 6, 10, 15 and 30

The highest number in both sets, i.e. the highest number that are common to both sets, is 6, so that's your Greatest Common Factor.

Least Common Multiple
=====================

Sometimes the term Least Common Multiple is called the Lowest Common Multiple or the Smallest Common Multiple or the Lowest Common Denominator when used in a fraction, but in any case, the concept is the same - without knowing this term, you can't compare, add, or subtract fractions, and that's important.

The least common multiple is the smallest number that can be divided by two (or more) given numbers. To get this number, first write out the multiples for each number and then find the smallest multiple that they share.

For example, find the Least Common Multiple of 3 and 7:

The multiples of 3 are: 3, 6, 9, 12, 15, 18, 21, 24, 27...
The multiples of 7 are: 7, 14, 21, 28, 35, 42, 49, 56...

The lowest number in both sets is 21, so that's your Least Common Multiple. Notice that there are other multiples, but we are interested in the lowest or least of the common multiples.

<u>Exponents and Roots</u>

Exponents:

An exponent is an algebraic operation that tells you to multiply a number by itself.

For example, 4^2 is the same as 4×4, and 4^3 is the same as $4 \times 4 \times 4$. The exponent tells you how many times to multiply the number by itself.

Exponents have a few special properties (you can think of them as shortcuts or even helpful tricks if you want):

1. If two numbers with exponents share the same base number, you can multiply them by adding the exponents:

$$2^5 \times 2^3 = 2^8$$

2. If two numbers with exponents share the same base number, you can divide them by subtracting the exponents:

$$2^5 \div 2^3 = 2^2$$

3. A number with an exponent raised to a negative power is the same as 1 over or the reciprocal of that number with an exponent raised to the positive power:

$$5^{-2} = 1/5^2$$

$$1/5^2 = 1/25 \text{ or } 1 \div 25 = 0.04$$

4. A number raised to a fraction power is the same as a root, or radical:

$$9^{1/2} = 3 \text{ (the square root indicated by the two in one half)}$$

Remember that the root of a number x is another number, which when multiplied by itself a given number of times, equals x. For example, the second root of 9 is 3, because $3 \times 3 = 9$. The second root is usually called the square root. The third root is usually called the cube root. Because $2 \times 2 \times 2 = 8$, 2 is the cube root of 8. Two special exponent properties are explained more in the two examples below.

1. 1 raised to any power is 1; for example:

$$1^2 = 1$$
$$1^{-4} = 1$$
$$1^{912} = 1$$

2. Any number raised to the power of 0 equals 1 — sounds crazy, but it's true! Here's an example:

$$253^0 = 1$$

If you can remember these six properties, you'll be able to simplify almost any problem with exponents.

Roots and Radicals

Roots and radicals are sometimes held up as cliché symbols for difficult math problems, but in the real world, they're easy to understand and use to solve equations.

A radical is an expression that has a square root, cube root, etc; the symbol is a $\sqrt{\ }$. The number under that radical sign is called a radicand.

A square is an expression (not an equation!) in which a number is multiplied by itself. It is often said that the given number is raised to the power of 2. Here's an example: 4^2 is a square. 4×4 is the same square, expressed differently.

ee

The square root of a number is a second number that, when multiplied by itself, will equal the first number. Therefore, it's the same as squaring a number, but in the opposite direction. For example, if you want to find the square root of 25, we have to figure out what number, when squared, equals 25. With enough experience, you will automatically know many of the common square roots. For example, it is commonly known that 5 is the square root of 25. Square and square root are operations that are often used to undo or cancel out each other in problem-solving situations.

A mental image, kind of like a numerical mnemonic, that helps some people is to think of the given number and the square root (in the above case, 25 and 5) as the tree and its much smaller roots in the ground.

The previous example uses the number 25, which is an example of a perfect square. Only some numbers are perfect squares – those that are equal to the product of two integers. Here's a table of the first 10 perfect squares.

Factors	Perfect Square
1x1	1
2x2	4
3x3	9
4x4	16
5x5	25
6x6	36
7x7	49
8x8	64
9x9	81
10x10	100

It is helpful to remember that if you find that the square root of any radicand is a whole number (not a fraction or a decimal), that means the given number is a perfect square.

To deal with radicals that are not perfect, you need to rewrite them as radical factors and simplify until you get one factor that's a perfect square. This process is sometimes called extracting or taking out the square root. This process would be used for the following number:

$$\sqrt{18}$$

First, it's necessary to notice that 18 has within it the perfect square 9.

$$18 = 9 \times 2 = 3^2 \times 2$$

Therefore, $\sqrt{18}$ is not in its simplest form. Now, you need to extract the square root of 9

$$\sqrt{18} = \sqrt{9} \times 2 = 3\sqrt{2}$$

Now the radicand no longer has any perfect square factors.

$\sqrt{2}$ is an irrational number that is equal to approximately 1.414. Therefore, the approximate answer is the following:

$$\sqrt{18} = 3 \times 1.414 = \text{approximately } 4.242$$

Note that the answer can only be an approximate one since $\sqrt{2}$ is an irrational number, which is any real number that cannot be expressed as a ratio of integers. Irrational numbers cannot be represented as terminating or repeating decimals.

Factorials

If you have ever seen a number followed by an exclamation point, it's not yelling at you – it's called a factorial. Simply put, a factorial is the product of a number and all of the positive integers below it, stopping at 1. For example, if you see 5!, its value is determined by doing the following example:

$$5! = 5 \times 4 \times 3 \times 2 \times 1 = 120$$

Factorials are typically used in relation to the fundamental principle of counting or for the combinations or permutations of sets.

Section 3: Decimals and Fractions

<u>Operations with Decimals</u>

The sign conventions for positive and negative decimal arithmetic operations are the same as those for whole number operations outlined in Module 1. But, there are special details to recall when performing arithmetic operations with decimal values to ensure correct answers.

When adding and subtracting decimal values, it is important to make sure that the decimal points are aligned vertically. This is the simplest method to ensure a reliable result. For example, adding 0.522 and 0.035 should be performed as follows:

$$
\begin{array}{r}
0.522 \\
+0.035 \\
\hline
0.557
\end{array}
$$

Subtraction operations should be aligned similarly.

$$
\begin{array}{r}
0.522 \\
-0.035 \\
\hline
0.487
\end{array}
$$

It is important to note that multiplication requires a different convention to be followed. When multiplying decimals, the operations are NOT aligned necessarily the same way as addition and subtraction. For example, multiplying 0.7 and 2.15 is performed as follows:

$$
\begin{array}{r}
2.15 \\
\times\, 0.7 \\
\hline
1.505
\end{array}
$$

When multiplying decimal values, the decimal point placement in the answer is determined by counting the total number of digits to the right of the decimal point in the multiplied numbers. This detail is often overlooked in testing choices where the same numbers may appear in several multiple-choice answers, but with different decimal point placements.

Division of decimal values is simplified by first visualizing fractions that are equivalent. The mathematics terminology is that a dividend / divisor = quotient. For example:

7.35 / 1.05 is the same as 73.5 / 10.5, which is the same operation as 735 / 105.

The last fraction, in the example above, means that to solve 7.35 / 1.05 we can divide 735 / 105 and find the correct whole number answer. This method just requires that when dividing by a decimal number, the divisor must be corrected to be a whole number. This requirement is achieved by moving the decimal points in **both the dividend and divisor** the same number of decimal places. If the dividend still contains a decimal point, the place is maintained in the long division operation, and the correct quotient is still achieved. The quotient remains in the form of a decimal number.

Operations with Fractions

The sign conventions for positive and negative fractional arithmetic operations are the same as those for whole number operations outlined in Module 1. However, there are special details to recall when performing arithmetic operations with fractional values to ensure correct answers.

Remember that fractions are made up of a numerator and a denominator. The top number of the fraction, called the numerator, tells how many of the fractional parts are being represented. The bottom number, called the denominator, tells how many equal parts the whole is divided into. For this reason, fractions with different denominators cannot be added together because different denominators are as different as "apples and oranges." So, when adding or subtracting fractions with different denominators, a common denominator must be found. In this case, simple geometric models will be used to explain the common denominator principle. Usually, this principle is illustrated with circles divided into "pie slices." A simpler and more effective example involves the use of squares or rectangles divided into fractional parts.

Representing fraction parts, $^1/_3$ and $^1/_4$ will be demonstrated with the following square diagrams. In this case a whole square is the number "1" and the fractional parts will be the slices of the square as follows:

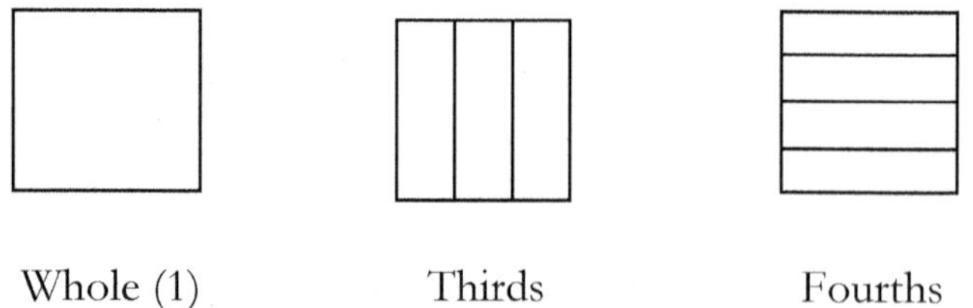

Whole (1)　　　　　Thirds　　　　　Fourths

If we superimpose the four horizontal slices over the three vertical slices, there are twelve separate parts of the whole as follows:

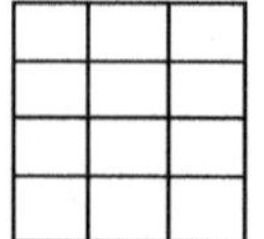

In the last diagram, any column representing a third, has four of the twelve small rectangles from the diagram, or $^4/_{12}$ as the equivalent fraction.

Similarly, any row of the last diagram, representing a fourth, has three of the twelve small rectangles from the diagram, or $^3/_{12}$ as the equivalent fraction. With this modification of the two fractions, both are now in the form of a common denominator, and the addition of the two fractions can be completed:

$$^1/_3 + {}^1/_4 = {}^3/_{12} + {}^4/_{12} = {}^7/_{12}$$

Notice that this result is exactly analogous to the simple diagram above. Common denominator fractions need not be simplified with this type of diagram, but it is a valuable example to explain the principle. The common denominator is required whenever adding or subtracting fractions with different denominators. If the denominators are the same, then the addition or subtraction of numerators is all that is required. If more assistance is needed on how to find common denominators, the Arithmetic Reasoning chapter in Module 1 will provide information on finding the Least Common Multiple, or the lowest common denominator, required for addition and subtraction. Remember that the individual fractions will retain the same value only if the numerator and denominator are multiplied by the same value.

Multiplication of fractions is a simple operation because fractions multiply as follows:

$$^7/_8 \times {}^3/_4 = {}^{(7*3)}/_{(8*4)} = {}^{21}/_{32}$$

This fraction is in its simplest form because there are no common factors. If common factors exist in the numerator and denominator of a fraction, then that fraction must be simplified.

Division of fractions should never be attempted in the form of a ratio. The method is confusing, elaborate and unreliable in a testing situation. Instead, **every** fraction division problem is a simple operation because the division operation can be rewritten as a multiplication operation. To begin, as stated previously:

$$\text{dividend} / \text{divisor} = \text{quotient}$$

This can be rewritten as:

$$\text{dividend} \times ({}^1/_{\text{divisor}}) = \text{quotient}$$

This yields exactly the same outcome as division. The quantity $({}^1/_{\text{divisor}})$ is called a reciprocal, and for a fraction, it's as simple as flipping the fraction upside down. Therefore:

$$({}^5/_8) / ({}^1/_4) = {}^5/_8 \times {}^4/_1 = {}^{20}/_{32} = {}^5/_8 \text{ (in simplified form)}$$

Fraction to Decimal Conversions

Every fraction represents a division problem. The decimal value of any fraction is represented by the numerator, (top value), divided by the denominator (bottom value). Certain combinations, such as $^1/_3$, will result in repeating decimals that will always be rounded in a multiple-choice testing situation.

The fraction $^1/_2$ has a decimal value of 0.5, which is the value of 1 divided by 2. The values of improper fractions such as $^3/_2$, $^5/_2$, or $^7/_2$ (larger numerator than denominator) are determined by dividing as previously stated or more easily by multiplying the numerator by 0.5. So the improper fraction of $^7/_2$ is 7×0.5, or 3.5. Often, the determination of the unit fraction (1 divided by the denominator) followed by the decimal multiplication is simpler in a testing situation.

The fraction $^3/_5$ has a decimal value of 0.6, which is the value of 3 divided by 5. Alternately, the value of the unit fraction of $^1/_5$ is 0.2, and that unit fraction multiplied by 3 is 0.6. If you know the unit fractions for common fraction values, the answer selection process may be simplified.

When a fraction such as $^5/_7$ is evaluated, the quotient of 5 divided by 7 results in a lengthy decimal value of 0.71428…. That extended value will never appear as a multiple-choice test answer selection. Typically, that value will be rounded to either 0.71 or 0.714. Remember that testing instructions say to choose the **best answer**. Your best choice may be a rounded number.

Decimal to Fraction Conversions

All decimals are also fractions and can be written in that form. The fractions that result all have powers of 10 in the denominator and usually need to be simplified in order to be compared to multiple-choice answers in a testing situation.

For example, simple decimal values, such as 0.25, can be written as the fraction $^{25}/_{100}$. This fraction must be simplified to be correct. $^{25}/_{100}$ can be rewritten as a product:

$$^{(25 * 1)}/_{(25 * 4)}$$

or

$$^{25}/_{25} \times {}^1/_4$$

The fraction can be expressed correctly as $^1/_4$ since the fraction $^{25}/_{25}$ is simplified to 1. Recognizing the common factors in the numerator and denominator is the essential element in making these conversions.

For testing purposes, decimal conversions will often be based on common fraction values. For example, $^1/_{16}$, if divided with long division, is 0.0625. Any integer multiple of this value results in a fraction with 16 in the denominator.

The value 0.0625 is first rewritten as the fraction:

$$625/10000$$

Simplifying with factors of 5 in the numerator and denominator gives the fraction

$$125/2000$$

Simplifying with factors of 25 in the numerator and denominator gives the fraction

$$5/80$$

Simplifying with factors of 5 in the numerator and denominator one more time gives the simplified fraction

$$1/16$$

While either of these methods may require an extra amount of time to complete, usually the answer choices may be logically reduced to two of the four examples. Testing the answer choices is simply a matter of multiplying the decimal value by the denominator to determine if the numerator is correct.

Another solution method, logical deduction, can be used as a simple, reliable and time saving approach to finding the fractional value of 0.435. In this example, the following is a list of possible multiple-choice answers:

A	$3/16$
B	$5/16$
C	$7/16$
D	$9/16$

Logically, any fraction greater than $1/2$ is immediately eliminated since:

$$0.435 < 0.5$$

So, first eliminate answer D. Incorrect answer choices will be eliminated with this type of logical deduction.

Second, notice that in the answer choice:

$$^3/_{16} < {}^1/_4$$

and in decimal form

$$^3/_{16} < 0.25$$

So, choice A can logically be eliminated since our answer comparison is with 0.435. Third, notice that in the answer choices:

$$^5/_{16} > {}^1/_4$$

and in decimal form

$$^5/_{16} > 0.25$$

Since $^5/_{16}$ is just slightly more than $^1/_4$, choice B can be eliminated since our comparison is with 0.435.

Finally, C is chosen as the most likely answer choice. It is the logical choice since:

$$^7/_{16} < {}^1/_2$$
$$\text{and}$$
$$0.435 < 0.5$$

Section 4: Percentages

Percentages is a concept you are most likely familiar with from real-world applications, so these are some of the less scary math problems that appear on tests. However, test writers take that confidence into account and can use it against you, so it's important to be careful on problems with percentages. Let's look at an example:

A sweater went on sale and now costs $25.20. If the original price was $42.00, what is the percent discount?

A 16.8%

B 20.0%

C 25.0%

D 40.0%

E 60.0%

Take a minute to work out the problem for yourself. If you get the wrong answer, it will be helpful to you to see where you went wrong – several of the answer choices are distinct traps that often appear on test questions like this.

Solution:

With percentages, you can always set up a fraction. First, you want to know what percent the sale price is of the original price. The reference point, or original price, will go on the bottom of the fraction. The numerator will be the sale price. The ratio of 25.2 / 42 is equal to 6 / 10. The sale price, $25.20, is 0.6, or 60%, of the original price. A percentage is just the decimal times 100.

This is answer choice E. However, the question did NOT ask what percent the new price is of the original price. Read carefully: it asks for the percent *discount*. This language is commonly used for questions with prices. Here's what it means, in math terms:

Percentage discount = 100% - Percentage of the Sale Price

The percent discount is the amount less than 100% that the sale price is of the original price. We can use this equation to solve, which yields: (42 – 25.2) / 42 = 0.40

Remember, a percent is a decimal times 100%. So, we can convert the decimal on the right side to a percentage by multiplying by 100%:

$$100\% \times 0.40 = 40\%$$

The sale price is 40% *less than* the original price, which is answer choice D. Another mathematical reasoning approach would be to take the original fraction subtracted from 1:

$$1 - 25.2 / 42 = 0.4$$

From here, just recognize that if the sale price *is* 60% of the original price, then it is 40% *less than* the original price.

You can solve for the discounted amount and then find that as a percent of the original amount to solve for the percentage of the discount:

$$42 - 25.2 = 16.80$$

$$16.80 / 42 = 0.4$$

Those are three different ways to approach one problem, using the same concept of percentage and recognizing that a percent *discount* requires subtraction from the original. Here's another percentage problem, this time with a different trick:

$$168 \text{ is } 120\% \text{ of what number?}$$

Solution:

First, convert 120% to a decimal. Remember, converting a percentage to a decimal is done by dividing by 100%:

$$120 / 100 = 1.2$$

We are told that 168 is this percent *of* some other number. This means that 168 goes in the numerator of our percent fraction equation. Here is the resulting equation:

$$168 / x = 1.2$$

Here, x signifies the unknown number in the problem. Writing the percent equation is indispensable to solving this type of problem. Multiply both sides by x and then divide both sides by 1.2 to isolate the variable:

$$168(x) / x = 1.2(x)$$

$$168 = 1.2x$$

$$168 / 1.2 = 1.2x / 1.2$$

$$140 = x$$

Therefore, 168 is 120% of 140. We can verify this answer by plugging the numbers back into the original equation:

$$168 / 140 = 1.2$$

This problem is tricky because the percentage is greater than 100%, or greater than 1.0, so it violates our intuition that the bigger number should go on the bottom of the fraction. Usually, percentages are less than 100. However, when percentages are larger than 100, the numerator is bigger than the denominator. The inverse of this question could be the following:

168 is what percent of 140?

Many people, after reading this question, would automatically set up the following fraction equation:

$$140/168 = 0.83$$

83% would likely be an answer choice, but it's the wrong answer. The question is asking for 168 / 140. Read these questions carefully, and don't automatically place the larger number in the denominator.

Let's look at one more example, which combines these concepts, and then do a couple practice problems:

An ingredient in a recipe is decreased by 20%. By what percentage does the new amount need to be increased to obtain the original amount of the ingredient?

Solution:

Here is a pro's tip for working with percentages:

When a problem is given only in percentages with no given numbers, you can substitute in any value to work with as your original amount. Since you are solving for a percent, you'll get the same answer no matter what numbers are used because percentages are ratios. The easiest number to work with in problems like this is 100, so use that as the original recipe amount. 100 what? Cups of flour? Chicken tenders? Chocolate chips? Doesn't matter. Here's how your equation should look:

$$x / 100 = 0.20$$

Solve for x, which gives the amount the ingredient has been decreased by:

$$x = 100 \times 0.20$$

Remember that 20% is a decimal, so $0.20 \times 100 = 20$. The ingredient has been decreased by 20 units. What is the new amount?

$$100 - 20 = 80$$

What was the question asking for? *By what percent does the new amount need to be increased to obtain the original amount of the ingredient?* Let's parse this mathematical language. We've found the new amount of the ingredient, 80. The original amount, we decided, was 100.

The next step in answering the question is to find the *amount* that we would need to add to get back to the original amount. This part is pretty easy:

$$80 + x = 100$$

$$x = 20$$

It's the same amount that we subtracted from the original amount, 20. But the question asks what percentage of 80 is required to add 20?

Set up the percentage equation. 80 times what percent (x / 100) will give that extra 20 units?

$$80 \times x / 100 = 20$$

Solve as normal by dividing both sides by 80 and then multiplying both sides by 100:

$$x / 100 = 0.25$$
$$x = 25$$

The new amount must be increased by 25% to equal the original amount.

Section 5: Rates and Systems of Equations

These are some of the most common questions on standardized math exams and also some of the most criticized. How many pop culture references are there to the nightmare of the "if train A is traveling west of Detroit at 70 km an hour and train B is traveling north of Denver at 90km an hour, what is the weight of the moon" variety? Excluding the nonsensical nature of the joke (would we weigh the moon in terms of its own gravity, or Earth's? Do bodies in orbit actually weigh *anything*?? Wait, wrong subject), this is simply a rate problem! Train A has a speed and a direction, Train B has a speed and a direction, and given those facts, you can answer all kinds of questions easily.

A *rate* is anything that relates two types of measurement: distance and time, dollars and workers, mass and volume, x per y. Exchange rates tell us how much of one currency you can get for a certain amount of another currency. Speedometers tell us how many kilometers we travel per unit of time. Growth rates tell us how much additional population we get over time. Rates are everywhere in the world, and they are everywhere on standardized math tests. To express a rate mathematically, think of the following:

All rates express one measurement *in terms of* another.

For example, *km per hour* gives us a measurement of distance (kilometers) for one unit of time (an hour). "Per" is a term that means divide. It looks like this:

If a car is traveling 40 kph, it goes 40 kilometers for every one hour of time that passes.

All rates work this way. If you can get €0.81 (Euros) for one American dollar, the exchange rate is:

€0.81 (Euros) / 1 Dollar = 0.81 Euros per Dollar

A rate is written as a fraction. A rate *equation* gives you a value of one of the measurements if you know the rate and the value of the other measurement.

If a car travels 40 kph: Distance = 40 km/hour × hours

This recipe for the equation always works for a rate problem:

Examine the mph example: when you multiply 40 km/hour times a number of hours, the hours units cancel out, leaving you with a number of kilometers. This works for any type of rate. The thing being measured on the *top* (numerator) of the rate measurement is equal to the rate times the unit being measured on the *bottom* of the rate measurement.

To solve a rate problem, follow these steps:

1. Read the question carefully to determine what you will be solving for. Is it an amount of time? A distance? Something else? Make sure you understand this before anything else. It can be helpful to name the variables at this point.

2. Write equations to express all of the information given in the problem. This is just like we've demonstrated for percentage problems, averaging problems, etc. The ability to express information in an equation is one of the main mathematical reasoning abilities that you can demonstrate to succeed on tests like these. Remember the equation:

$$\text{Distance} = \text{Rate} \times \text{Time}$$

3. Solve!

First, a simple example:

A train is traveling west at 75 km/h. How long will it take to travel 60 kilometers?

Step 1: Identify what the question is asking for: in this instance, it's *how long*, or the time it takes to travel 60 kilometers.

Step 2: Write an equation: $60 = 75 \times \text{time}$

Step 3: Solve! We know that the rate is 75 kilometers per hour and that the km traveled is 60. To solve for time, just plug those values into the equation:

Isolate the "x hours" by dividing both sides by 75 km/h:

$$60 \text{ kilometers} / 75 \text{ km per hour} = 0.8 \text{ hours}$$
$$0.8 \text{ hours} \times 60 \text{ minutes per hour} = 48 \text{ minutes}$$

Rate problems can also require a system of equations. This just means that you need to write two equations to relate two unknown variables, instead of one equation to solve for one unknown variable, like the problem above. The algebra is not any more difficult for these types of problems. They just require the extra step of writing another equation.

For example: Jessica assembles one model airplane per hour. James assembles one model airplane per 45 minutes. If they work for the same amount of time and assemble twelve planes all together, how many planes did James assemble?

Step 1: Identify what the question is asking for: the number of planes that James assembled.

Step 2: Write equations:

$$x = 1 \text{ Airplanes per hour} \times T \text{ hours}$$
$$y = 1/0.75 \text{ Airplanes per hour} \times T \text{ hours}$$
$$x + y = 12$$

You convert "45 minutes" to 0.75 hours, since $45/60 = 0.75$. If you'd rather not do that, you could leave the rate in minutes, but then change Jessica's rate to 60 minutes instead of one hour. The important thing is to use the same units for time across the whole equation.

Step 3: Solve! Notice that the "T hours" term is the same in both of the rate equations. The problem stated that the two of them worked for the same amount of time. To solve for the number of planes James assembled, first we need to find T hours. The *number of planes Jessica assembles* and the *number of planes James assembles* can be added together since we know that the sum is 12. This is the new equation from adding those together:

$$12 = 1 \text{ Airplanes per hour} \times T \text{ hours} + 1/0.75 \text{ Airplanes per hour} \times T \text{ hours}$$

The algebra here is a little bit hairy, but we can handle it! To solve for time, isolate T step by step. First, multiply every term in the equation by "1 hour":

Now, the unit "hour" cancels out of both terms on the right side of the equation. Remember, when you multiply *and* divide a term by something, that cancels out:

$$12 \, planes \times (1 \, hour)$$
$$= \cancel{(1 \, hour)} \times \frac{1 \, plane}{\cancel{1 \, hour}} \times T \, hours + \cancel{(1 \, hour)} \times \frac{1 \, plane}{0.75 \, \cancel{hours}} \times T \, hours$$

Now, we have:

$$12 \text{ plane hours} = 1 \text{ plane} \times T \text{ hours} + 1/0.75 \times T \text{ hours}$$

We need to isolate "T hours." Gather together the "T hours" terms on the right side of the equation. Right now, they are separated into an addition expression. If we add them together, they will be collected into one term. Since $1/0.75$ is equal to $4/3$, change that term first:

$$12 \text{ plane hours} = 1 \text{ plane} \times T \text{ hours} + 4/3 \text{ plane} \times T \text{ hours}$$

Now add:

$$12 \text{ plane hours} = (1 \text{ plane} + 4/3 \text{ plane}) \times \text{T hours}$$
$$12 \text{ plane hours} = (1 \text{ and } 4/3 \text{ plane}) \times \text{T hours}$$

You add together 1 and 4/3. This is the same as saying that $1x + 2x = 3x$. We just collected the like terms.

Now, divide both sides by 1 plane to isolate the T hours term. Since mixed fractions are difficult to work with, change this into an improper fraction:

$$12 \text{ plane hours} = (7/3 \text{ plane}) \times \text{T hours}$$

The planes unit cancels out on the right side. So we are left with:

$$12 \text{ hours} / (7/3) = \text{T hours}$$

One arithmetic trick: dividing by a fraction is the same as multiplying by the inverse of the fraction. If you are comfortable dividing by fractions on your calculator, you can do the rest of the problem that way, or else you can flip the fraction over and simplify the arithmetic:

$$12 \times 3/7 = \text{T hours}$$
$$36/7 = \text{T hours}$$
$$5 \ 1/7 = \text{T hours}$$

The answer is $x = 5 \ {}^{1}/_{7}$ hours, or approximately 5.14 hours.

That was a long problem! But it included rates, a system of equations, unit conversions (changing minutes into fractions of an hour) and algebra with complex fractions. That is about the most difficult type of rate problem you would ever see on a standardized math exam, so if you were able to follow along with the solution you're in good shape.

Remember, on exams like this, the vast majority of points come from the easier problems. The harder problems (which on most exams tend to be at the end of a section) are always worth giving a shot, but they are not necessary to get a good score. Problems like these are great for practice because they include a lot of different concepts. Don't be discouraged if you don't always get the tougher problems correct on the first try. They are preparing you to do well on a wide range of different problem types!

Section 6: Sets

<u>Working with Sets</u>

All standardized math exams will touch on the basic statistical descriptions of sets of numbers: mean (the same as an average, for a set), median, mode and range. These are terms to know. Let's look at an example set and examine what each of these terms means:

Set of numbers: 42, 18, 21, 26, 22, 21

Mean

The mean of a set of numbers is the average value of the set. The formula for finding the mean is:

$$\frac{Sum\ of\ the\ numbers\ in\ the\ set}{Quantity\ of\ numbers\ in\ the\ set} = mean$$

Use this formula to find the mean of the example set:

$$\frac{42 + 18 + 21 + 26 + 22 + 21}{6} = \frac{150}{6} = 25$$

You add together all the numbers that appear in the set, and then divide by the quantity of numbers in the set. The mean, or average, value in the set is 25. Notice that the mean is not necessarily a number that appears in the set, although it can be.

Median

The median of a set is the number that appears in the middle **when the set is ordered from least to greatest.** Therefore, the first step in finding the mean is to put the numbers in the correct order, if they are not already. You should always do this physically, on your scratch paper, to make sure that you don't leave any numbers out of the reordering. For the example set, that would be:

18, 21, 21, 22, 26, 42

Make sure you've included all the numbers in the order, even if there are duplicates. If a set with a lot of numbers, it's helpful to cross them off in the original set as you order them on your scratch paper. This helps ensure that you don't leave one out.

If there is an odd quantity of numbers in the set, the median will be the middle number. For example, if a set is comprised of nine numbers, the median will be the fifth number of the ordered set.

However, the example set has six numbers. Since no single number is in the exact middle, we average the two middle numbers to find the median:

$$\frac{21 + 22}{2} = 21.5$$

The median of this set is 21.5.

Mode

The mode of a set of numbers is the number that appears most often. Speakers of French will find this easy to remember: *mode* is the French word for style. The number that appears the most is "in style" for this particular set.

The example set has one number that appears more than once: 21. Therefore, 21 is the mode. Sometimes, it's easiest to see this after the set is ordered, when duplicate numbers appear next to one another.

If a set has two numbers that equally appear most often, such as two 21s and two 22s, then both 21 *and* 22 are the mode. We don't average them together, as we do to find the median. Therefore, the mode is the only descriptor of a set that must always be a number in the set. Since there are two modes, the set would be described as "bimodal."

Range

The range of a set of numbers is the distance between the highest and lowest values. Once you've reordered a set, these values are easy to identify. Simply subtract the two values to get the range:

$$Highest\ value - Lowest\ value = Range$$

For the example set, this would be:

$$42 - 18 = 24$$

The range of the set is 24.

Sets can include negative numbers, decimals, fractions, duplicates, etc. They may also appear in table form. Let's look at another example set to see what kinds of tricky questions you may encounter.

Month	Rainfall (cm)
August	0.8
September	1.3
October	2.1
November	1.3
December	3.7

What is the average rainfall for the months September, October, November and December?

Solution:

Notice the first trick in this question – you are asked for the average of only four months, not all five listed in the table. This introduces two possible sources of error – you could add all five months' rainfall and/or divide by five when calculating the average. To find the average of only the four months stated in the question, the solution is:

$$\frac{1.3 + 2.1 + 1.3 + 3.7}{4} = 2.1 \; cm$$

Here's another question for the same data table, but it uses a different approach to averaging:

The average monthly rainfall from July through December was 1.7 cm. What was the rainfall, in centimeters, in July?

Solution:

This question gives you the average and asks you to find the missing rainfall value. This is a common way to make a mean/average problem a little tricky for the average (mean) test-taker. You can solve these types of questions by applying the basic equation for finding the mean:

$$\frac{Sum \; of \; the \; numbers \; in \; the \; set}{Quantity \; of \; numbers \; in \; the \; set} = mean$$

Next, fill in all the known values:

$$\frac{July + 0.8 + 1.3 + 2.1 + 1.3 + 3.7}{6} = 1.7$$

Solve algebraically:

$$July + 0.8 + 1.3 + 2.1 + 1.3 + 3.7 = 1.7 \times 6$$

$$July = (1.7 \times 6) - 0.8 - 1.3 - 2.1 - 1.3 - 3.7$$

$$July = 1 \; inch$$

Now, try to solve this question:

> What is the difference between the mode and the median of the rainfalls for August through December?

Solution:

Simply find the mode and median values. Remember, the first step is to order the set:

$$0.8, 1.3, 1.3, 2.1, 3.7$$

The mode is 1.3 because that is the only number that appears more than once.

The median is 1.3 because, of the five numbers in the set, 1.3 is the third (middle) number.

Therefore, the difference between the mode and the median is:

$$1.3 - 1.3 = 0$$

Section 7: Probability and Ratios

<u>Probability</u>

Every probability is a ratio as described below.

$$\text{Probability} = \frac{\text{Total number of desired events}}{\text{Total number of possible outcomes}}$$

The simplest example of this type of ratio is found when tossing a coin. There are always two total outcomes, heads and tails, so the probability of either a head or a tail is always 1/2 for that coin.

Similarly, if you tossed that same coin 14 times, you would expect to see it land 7 times with the head showing and 7 times with the tail showing. Because these events are totally random, flipping the coin 14 times will not always provide an equal number of outcomes in a group of trials. So we say that the number of heads in a trial of 14 is the "expected value" of 7. Similarly, 7 would be the "expected value" for tails.

A common misconception is that there "has to be" a certain outcome based on the number of outcomes that have already occurred. In the repeated trial of an event, each outcome is its own trial and is not influenced by the previous trial or trials.

The other common type of probability problem is with dice, where each of six faces of a cube has its own number from 1 to 6. Each of these numbers has the probability of 1/6 for a single roll of the die.

If we formulate a table of outcomes for two dice, thrown together, the details are slightly different. In this table, the individual numbers are shown across the top and vertically along the side. The entries in the table represent the total of the two dice.

	1	2	3	4	5	6	Cube "A"
1	2	3	4	5	6	7	
2	3	4	5	6	7	8	
3	4	5	6	7	8	9	
4	5	6	7	8	9	10	
5	6	7	8	9	10	11	
6	7	8	9	10	11	12	

Cube "B"

A look at the table shows that there are 36 possible outcomes when two dice are thrown together (6×6). The individual probabilities are shown below.

P (1) = 0 (never appears)

P (2) = $^1/_{36}$ does not simplify (appears once)

P (3) = $^2/_{36}$ simplifies to $^1/_{18}$ (appears twice)

P (4) = $^3/_{36}$ simplifies to $^1/_{12}$ (appears three times)

P (5) = $^4/_{36}$ simplifies to $^1/_9$ (appears four times)

P (6) = $^5/_{36}$ does not simplify (appears five times)

P (7) = $^6/_{36}$ simplifies to $^1/_6$ (appears six times)

P (8) = $^5/_{36}$ does not simplify (appears five times)

P (9) = $^4/_{36}$ simplifies to $^1/_9$ (appears four times)

P (10) = $^3/_{36}$ simplifies to $^1/_{12}$ (appears three times)

P (11) = $^2/_{36}$ simplifies to $^1/_{18}$ (appears twice)

P (12) = $^1/_{36}$ does not simplify (appears once)

P (13) = 0 (never occurs)

The symmetry of the table helps us visualize the probability ratios for the individual outcomes. By the definition of probability, any number larger than 13 will never appear in the table so the probability has to be zero. The probability of any impossible outcome always has to be zero. By the same reasoning, any event that must happen will have a probability of one. So, the probability of rolling a number from 2 to 12 is one.

If you are finding the probability of two events happening, the individual probabilities are added. For example, the probability of rolling a ten or eleven is the same as the probability of rolling an eight. The number eight appears in the table the same number of times as the combined total of appearances of ten or eleven.

The formulation of ratios for probabilities is simplest when using fractions. Often, the expression of a probability answer will be in a percent or a decimal. A coin from the first example would have the following probabilities P (heads) = 50% or .5 or 0.5.

Formulating probabilities from a word problem can always be structured around the ratio defined at the beginning of this section. However, the words can mislead or misdirect problem-solving efforts.

For example, a problem that describes a class distribution may often be stated as the number of boys and the number of girls. The probability of selecting a boy in a random sample is defined as the number of boys divided by the TOTAL number of boys AND girls. This is simple to see, but problems can be worded to mislead you into selecting the incorrect answer or to lead to the wrong conclusion when calculating an answer.

Another way that probability problems can be misleading is when multiple choices are used when simplified ratios are required. For example, if a class is made up of 6 girls and 10 boys, the probability of randomly selecting a girl from the classroom is $^{6}/_{16}$ or $^{3}/_{8}$. The misleading multiple choices that may be listed would often include 60%, (6/10) or 50% (since there are two outcomes — boys and girls). Reading a probability problem carefully is extremely important in both formulating the probability ratio and in making sure that the correct ratio is selected in the correct form. If the probability ratio for the example is formulated as $^{6}/_{16}$, the simplified form of $^{3}/_{8}$ is the only correct answer.

Ratios and Proportions

Ratios and fractions are synonymous when discussing numerical values. The ratios or fractions always imply division of the numerator by the denominator. In this section, the discussion is directed toward how words appear in ratio problems and how those words should be interpreted.

A commonly used ratio is contained in the term "kilometers per hour", usually abbreviated by km/h. When the term "kilometers per hour" is interpreted numerically, it is the ratio of the total number of kilometers traveled divided by the number of hours traveled. The key word in this commonly used term is "per". It literally means for each hour of travel a specific number of kilometers will be traveled. It has the same implication when the term is "gallons per hour" (how fast a tub is filled or a lawn is watered) or "tons per year" (how much ore is mined in one year).

Another way that ratios can appear is when a phrase defines a ratio as one value to another. A commonly used comparison is usually the ratio of "men to women" or "boys to girls". When this terminology is used, the first term is in the numerator, and the second term is in the denominator by convention.

There is an inherent problem when this terminology is used as illustrated by the example below:

> In a classroom setting, the ratio of girls to boys is 3 to 4 (or 3:4 in strictly mathematical terms). How many boys are there in the classroom if the total number of students is 28?

There are two ways that this word problem may be easily solved. If the ratio of ($^{girls}/_{boys}$) is ¾, the actual numbers may be ¾ or $^{6}/_{8}$ or $^{9}/_{12}$ or $^{12}/_{16}$ and so forth. These fractions are all equivalent fractions since they all simplify to the value of ¾. The equivalent fractions are easily determined as the ratios of multiples of the numerator and denominator of the original fraction. There is only one fraction where the numerator and denominator add to 28, and that is the ratio $^{12}/_{16}$. Therefore, the solution is the classroom has 16 boys and 12 girls.

Notice that the words specify which group (boys or girls) is the numerator and denominator in the original problem and in the solution. When choosing multiple-choice answers, make sure that the correct answer is chosen based upon the wording in the original problem. Most often, the correct ratio and its reciprocal are in the answer choices. For example, if the sample problem appeared on the exam, the multiple-choice answers would most likely include 16 boys and 12 girls AND 12 boys and 16 girls. But 16 boys and 12 girls is the correct answer choice.

Section 8: Scientific Notation

Scientific notation was originally developed as a simplified way for scientists to express extremely large or small numbers. In mathematics, scientific notation is used to easily compare large and small numbers. Let's take a look at how to translate a real number to its scientific notation equivalent.

Converting standard numbers to scientific notation is performed without calculation, although counting place values is still essential. For example:

> The number 2,345,000 is equal to 2.345 $\times$ 1,000,000. By writing the value of 1,000,000 as 10^6 (10 multiplied by itself 6 times), the formulation of the scientific notation equivalent of the original number is completed: 2.345 $\times$ 10^6.

Similarly, small decimal numbers can be written using scientific notation as well. For example:

> The number 0.00736 is equal to 7.36 $\times$ 0.001. By writing the value of 0.001 as 10^{-3} (1 divided by 10, three times), the formulation of the scientific notation equivalent of the original number is completed: 7.36 $\times$ 10^{-3}.

Instead dividing (or multiplying) by 10, the translation to scientific notation can also be simplified by counting the number of places that the decimal point is transferred in the conversion process. In the first example above, when the scientific notation was written, it began with writing 2.345. This number was formulated by moving the decimal point six places to the left in the original number. Therefore, the exponent of 10 was 6 (10^6).

Similarly, in the second example, the decimal part of the scientific notation number, 7.36, was written by moving the decimal point three places to the right. Therefore, the exponent of 10 was -3 (10^{-3}).

Using this method, no calculation is required. The included benefit is that the "significance" of numbers is easily determined. Answering the question of the number of significant figures for the two examples is a simple matter when using scientific notation. The number of digits in the decimal part of the scientific notation is always the number of significant figures. 2,345,000 has four significant figures. 0.00736 has three. The zeros in these numbers are often referred to as "place holders" when converting to scientific notation.

Notice that the exponent is NOT determined by counting zeros, but by counting the number of decimal places that are moved when formulating the scientific notation. The decimal part in scientific notation always has only one digit to the left of the decimal point.

Section9: Geometry

To tackle geometry questions on a mathematical reasoning test, there are a few formulas and rules that you need to know. This section takes you through those basic rules. It covers intersecting lines, triangles, squares and rectangles, and circles.

Basic Vocabulary

Vocabulary that is important to know for geometry questions includes the following:

Line – A line is a set of all points between two endpoints. Lines have no area or width, only length.

Angle – An angle is the corner formed by two intersecting line segments, and it is measured in degrees. Degrees measurements show the magnitude of the "sweep" of the angle. In the figure below, angle x is shown as the measure between the two line segments.

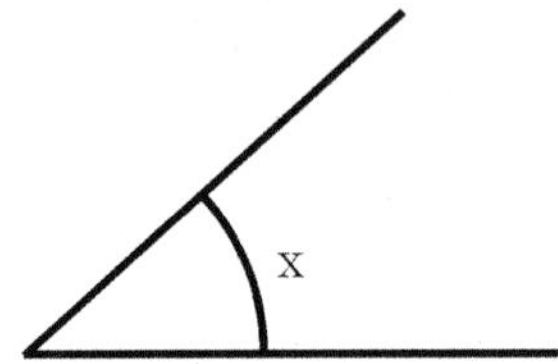

$360°$ describes the angle measurement all the way around a full circle. Half of that, $180°$, is the angle measurement across a straight line. Two lines at right angles to each other, called perpendicular lines, have an angle measurement of $90°$.

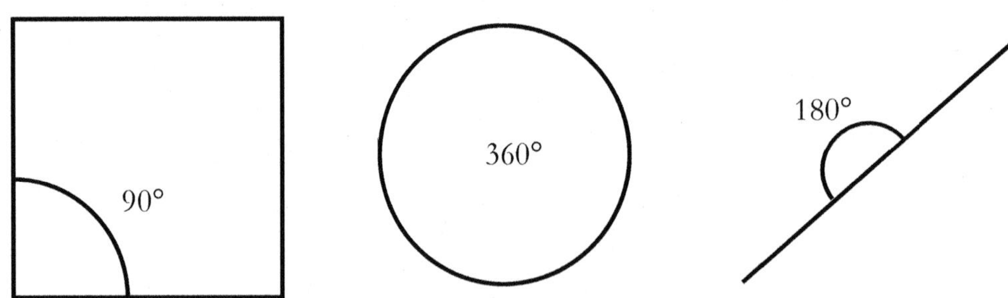

Area – The area is the measure of space inside a two-dimensional figure. It has units of length × length, or $length^2$. For example, rooms are described as being a number of square meters. Counties are described as being so many square kilometers. Each basic shape has a special formula for determining area.

Perimeter – The perimeter is the measure of the length around the outside of a figure.

Volume – For three-dimensional figures, the volume is the measure of space inside the figure. Volume has three dimensions: length $\times$ width $\times$ height. Because of this, it has units of length^3 (cubic length). For example, you may have heard "cubic meters" used to describe the volume of something like a storage unit. This formula applies only to square and rectangular three-dimensional shapes. Other figures have their own formulas for determining volume.

Intersecting Lines

There are two important properties to know about pairs of intersecting lines:

1. They form angles that add up to 180° along the sides of each line.
2. They create two pairs of equal angles.

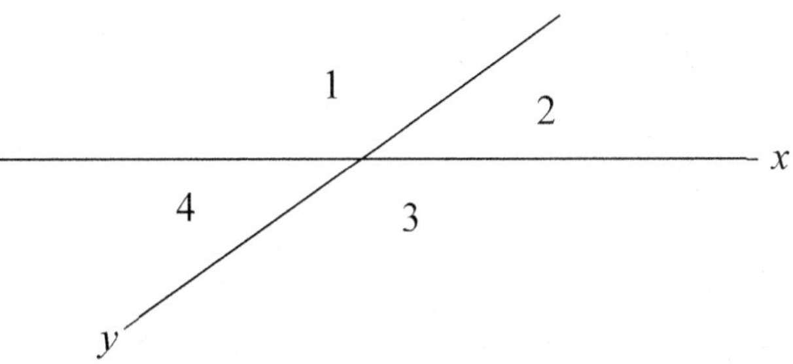

For example, in the diagram above, line x intersects line y, forming the four angles 1, 2, 3 and 4. Any two angles along one side of a line will add up to 180°:

$$Angle\ 1 + Angle\ 2 = 180°$$
$$Angle\ 2 + Angle\ 3 = 180°$$
$$Angle\ 3 + Angle\ 4 = 180°$$
$$Angle\ 4 + Angle\ 1 = 180°$$

All four of the angles added together would equal 360°:

$$Angle\ 1 + Angle\ 2 + Angle\ 3 + Angle\ 4 = 360°$$

The two angles DIAGONAL from each other must be equal. For the figure above, we know that:

$$Angle\ 1 = Angle\ 3$$
$$Angle\ 2 = Angle\ 4$$

This property is very useful: if you are given any one of the angles, you can immediately solve for the other three. If you are told that Angle 1 = 120°, then you know that Angle 2 = 180° - 120° = 60°. Since Angle 3 = Angle 1 and Angle 4 = Angle 2, you now know all four angles.

Parallel/Perpendicular Lines

Parallel lines are lines that lie on the same 2-D plane (i.e., the page) and never intersect each other. The thing to remember about parallel lines is that if a line intersects two parallel lines, it will form a bunch of corresponding angles (like the ones discussed above). Also, you can never assume that two lines are parallel just from a diagram. You need to be told or given enough information that you can deduce it. Parallel lines have the same slope.

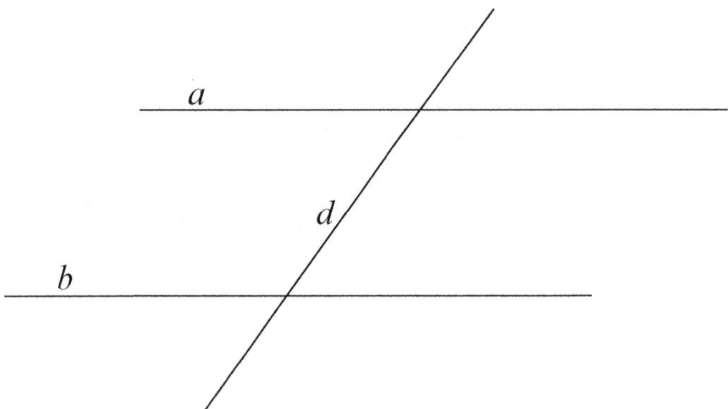

Lines *a* and *b* are parallel and are intersected by line *d*.

In the diagram above, all four of the acute angles (the ones smaller than 90°) are equal to each other. All four of the obtuse angles (the ones greater than 90°) are equal to each other. Why? Because a line intersecting parallel lines forms equivalent angles. This is simply an expanded case of the intersecting lines concept discussed earlier.

Squares and Rectangles

By definition, a square has four sides of equal length and four angles of 90°. A rectangle has two pairs of sides of equal length and four angles of 90°. This means that the sum of all four angles in a square or rectangle is 360°.

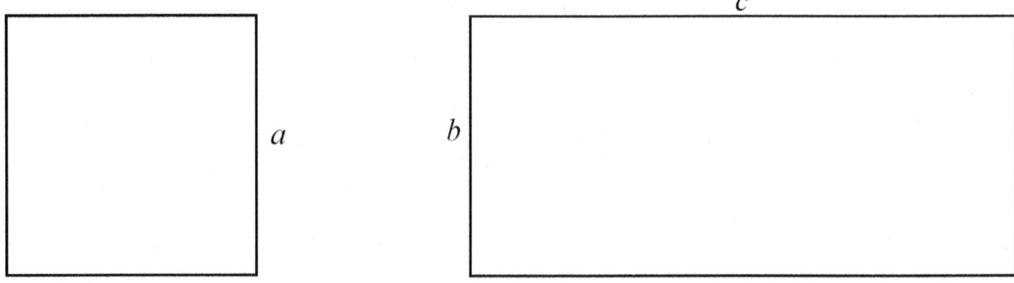

In the diagram above, the shape on the left is a square. So, if you are given the length of side *a*, you automatically know the length of every side. You already know the measure of every angle, because they are all 90° - the measure of right (perpendicular) angles.

The shape on the right is a rectangle. So, if you are given the length of side b, you know the length of the opposite side. However, you do not know the length of the longer two sides unless they are given.

The **perimeter** of a square is the sum of all four line segments. Since the line segments are equal, the equation is as follows:

$$Perimeter\ of\ a\ square = 4 \times (side\ length)$$

The perimeter of the square above is $4a$.

The perimeter of the rectangle is also the sum of its sides. However, since there are two pairs of equal length sides in a rectangle, the equation is as follows:

$$Perimeter\ of\ a\ rectangle = 2 \times (long\ side\ length) + 2 \times (short\ side\ length)$$

The perimeter of the rectangle above is $2b + 2c$.

The **area** of a square is its length times its width. Since length and width are the same for a square, the area is the length of one of its sides squared (that's where the term "squared" comes from) and the equation is as follows:

$$Area = a^2$$

For a rectangle, length times width is not equal to one side squared (it's not a square, so the sides are not all the same length). The equation for the area of a rectangle is as follows:

$$Area = b \times c$$

<u>Triangles</u>

A triangle is a polygon (closed shape) made of three line segments. While the four angles in a square and rectangle always add up to 360°, the three angles in a triangle always add up to 180°.

However, these angles are not always the same measure, as they are for squares and rectangles.

Below are the different types of triangles:

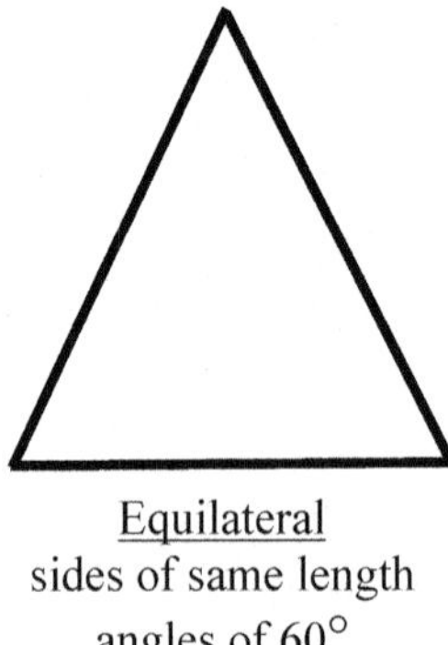 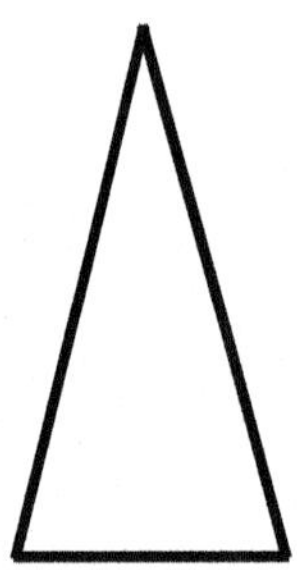 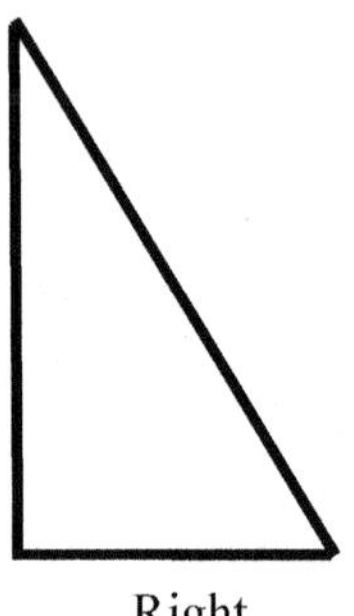

<u>Equilateral</u>
sides of same length
angles of 60°

<u>Isosceles</u>
two sides of same length
two angles of same measure

<u>Right</u>
one angle of 90°

The area of a triangle will always equal one half of the product of its base and its height. You can choose any side to be the base (the one at the bottom of the triangle is probably best), and the height of a triangle is the perpendicular line from the base to the opposite angle. The height is NOT the length of a side, unless the triangle is a right triangle. For example:

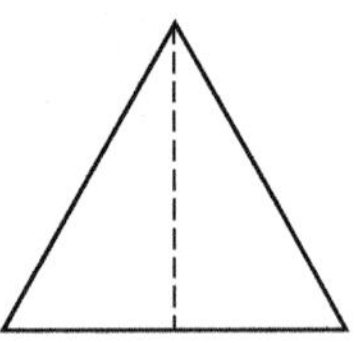

In this triangle, the bottom leg is the base, and the dotted line is the height.

$$A = \frac{1}{2} \, (base \times height)$$

Another important formula to know when working with triangles is the Pythagorean Theorem. This tells you how to relate the lengths of the sides of right triangles – the ones that include 90° angles.

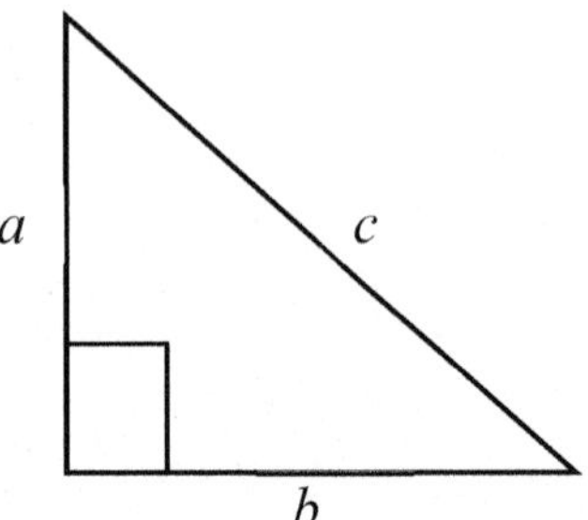

In the diagram above, you have right triangle ABC. You know it's a right triangle because it has a 90° angle – not because it *looks* like one. Never assume the measure of an angle without being given that information. Side c is called the hypotenuse, which is the longest side of a right triangle. Sides a, b and c are related to each other according to the Pythagorean Theorem:

$$c^2 = a^2 + b^2$$

Regardless of how the sides of the right triangle are labeled, the length of the longest side squared is equal to the sum of the lengths of the two shorter sides, each squared. There will likely be a few problems that will require you to use this relationship to solve.

Here are some important details to remember about triangles:
- A triangle has three sides and three angles.
- The angles of a triangle will always add up to 180°.
- A triangle is a "right triangle" if one of the angles is 90°.
- If a triangle is equilateral, all angles are 60°, and all sides are the same length.
- The area of a triangle is one half times the base times the height.
- For right triangles, you can relate the lengths of the sides using the Pythagorean Theorem.

Circles

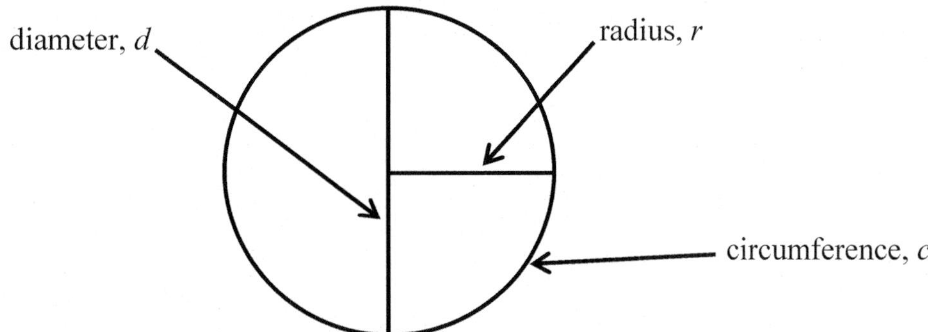

A circle is a figure without sides. Instead, it has a circumference with a set of points equidistant from the center of the circle.

Here are some important details to remember about circles:
- The measurement around the outside of a circle is called the **circumference**.
- The line segment going from the center of the circle to the circumference is called the **radius**.

- The line segment that goes across the entire circle, passing through the center, is the **diameter**.
- The number of degrees in the central angle of a circle is 360°.

The circumference of a circle can be found using the following formula:

$$C = 2\pi r$$

In this formula, r is the radius (or the distance from the center of the circle to an outside point on the circle). If you are given the diameter, then you can find the circumference using this formula:

$$C = \pi d$$

The radius is twice the length of the diameter:

$$D = 2r$$

The area of a circle can be found using this formula:

$$A = \pi r^2$$

So, the area is equal to the radius squared times the constant π (pronounced pi). Sometimes, answer choices are given with π as a part of the value, 2π, for example. When you see this, work out the problem without substituting the value of π (approximately 3.14). You can, in fact, estimate that π is 3.14 or 22/7 in your calculations, but you'll end up with a decimal or fraction for your answer.

Section 10: Trigonometry

<u>Right Triangle Trigonometry</u>
Trigonometry about a right triangle involves the ratio of any two sides of a right triangle *relative to the angle.* The side you call "OPP" (for opposite) must be opposite wherever your angle is located. The "HYP" side (for hypotenuse) is always opposite the right angle. The third side is then called "ADJ" (for adjacent). *It helps to identify the sides in this order.*

"sin" stands for "sine", "cos" stands for "cosine" and "tan" stands for "tangent". A common acronym used to remember the rules is SOH-CAH-TOA:

Sine = Opp/Hyp   Cosine = Adj/Hyp   Tangent = Opp / Adj

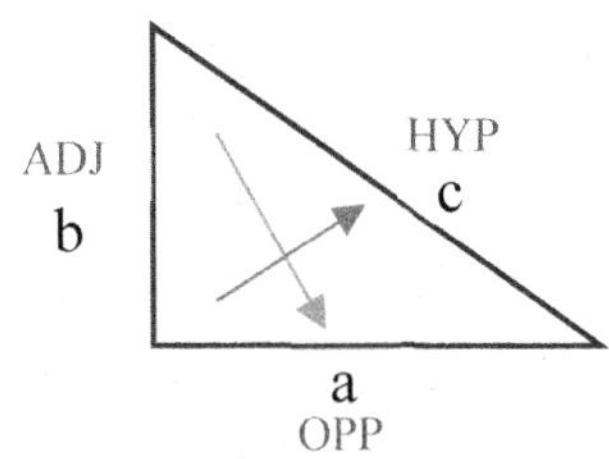

$$sin\alpha = \frac{opp}{hyp} = \frac{a}{c}$$
$$cos\alpha = \frac{adj}{hyp} = \frac{b}{c}$$
$$tan\alpha = \frac{opp}{adj} = \frac{a}{b}$$

$$sin\beta = \frac{opp}{hyp} = \frac{b}{c}$$
$$cos\beta = \frac{adj}{hyp} = \frac{a}{c}$$
$$tan\beta = \frac{opp}{adj} = \frac{b}{a}$$

There are 6 trigonometry functions. Each of the three main ones has its own reciprocal function as follows from the left triangle above:

$$sin\alpha = \frac{opp}{hyp} = \frac{a}{c} \qquad csc\alpha = \frac{hyp}{opp} = \frac{c}{a}$$ ← "csc" stands for "cosecant "

$$cos\alpha = \frac{adj}{hyp} = \frac{b}{c} \longleftrightarrow sec\alpha = \frac{hyp}{opp} = \frac{c}{b}$$ ← "sec" stands for "secant"

$$tan\alpha = \frac{opp}{adj} = \frac{a}{b} \longleftrightarrow cot\alpha = \frac{opp}{adj} = \frac{b}{a}$$ ← "cot" stands for "cotangent"

HELPFUL TIP: When practicing, write each function next to its reciprocal like this to remember which functions are reciprocals of each other. Knowing two functions are reciprocals will help with many problems!

Example 1: Find all six trigonometric function values of acute angle α for the triangle given. Then, use the values to evaluate the expression

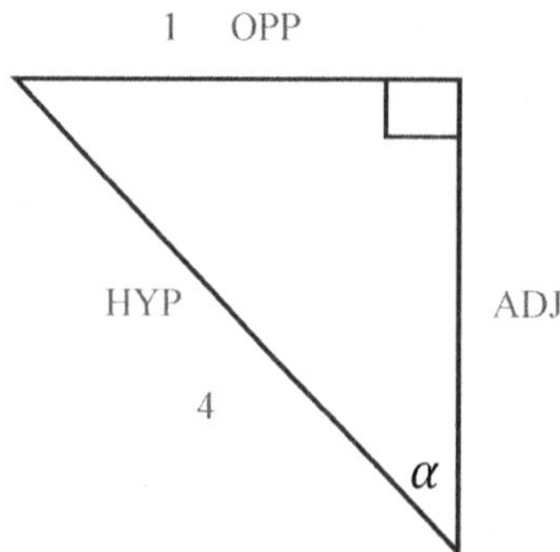

Step 1: Label each side, making sure the side across from your angle is "opp" and the side across from the right angle is "hyp".

Step 2: Find your missing side with the Pythagorean Theorem, making sure the hypotenuse is alone in the equation. $(1)^2 + (adj)^2 = (4)^2$ ➔ $(adj)^2 = 16 - 1$ ➔ $adj = \pm\sqrt{15}$. Since the angle is acute, it's in the first quadrant in standard position and all trigonometric functions are positive in the first quadrant. Therefore, $adj = +\sqrt{15}$.

Step 3: Use SOH-CAH-TOA and the right triangle trigonometry definition for your ratios:

$$sin\alpha = \frac{1}{4} \qquad\qquad csc\alpha = \frac{4}{1} = 4$$

$$cos\alpha = \frac{\sqrt{15}}{4} \qquad\qquad sec\alpha = \frac{4}{\sqrt{15}}\frac{\sqrt{15}}{\sqrt{15}} = \frac{4\sqrt{15}}{15}$$

$$tan\alpha = \frac{1}{\sqrt{15}}\frac{\sqrt{15}}{\sqrt{15}} = \frac{\sqrt{15}}{15} \qquad\qquad cot\alpha = \frac{\sqrt{15}}{1} = \sqrt{15}$$

Step 4: To evaluate an expression, substitute the values in for each and simplify.

$$2(csc\alpha) - 8(cos\alpha) + 6(tan\alpha)$$

$$= 2(4) - 8\left(\frac{\sqrt{15}}{4}\right) + 6\left(\frac{\sqrt{15}}{15}\right) = 8 - 2\sqrt{15} + \frac{2\sqrt{15}}{5}$$

$$= 8 - \frac{10\sqrt{15}}{5} + \frac{2\sqrt{15}}{5} = 8 - \frac{8\sqrt{15}}{5} = \frac{40 - 8\sqrt{15}}{5}$$

Example 2: Your friend throws you a 50 meter rope from the top of a building and puts his end at his feet. You measure the angle at your feet up to your friend to be 42°. How tall is the building?

50m

x   42°

Step 1: Label a diagram with appropriate measurements. Figure out which sides (opp, hyp, adj) are given relative to the 42° angle.

Step 2: Since "x" is the opposite side and "50 m" is the hypotenuse, you can either use "sine" or "cosecant". Both are correct, but your calculator only has the sine button, so that would be easier.

$$sin42° = \frac{opp}{hyp} = \frac{x}{50}$$

Step 3: Isolate the variable by multiplying both sides by 50:

$$(50)\, sin42° = \frac{x}{50}(50) \; \rightarrow \; x = 50sin42° \approx 34 \text{ ft}$$

Rounding Note: Always check what the directions specify for rounding. If no rounding is specified, follow suit with what is given in the problem. This problem gave whole numbers, so a matching whole-number answer is given.

Calculator tip: Always remember to check you're in the correct mode on your calculator. This problem would require degree mode since the angle is given in degrees.

<u>Oblique Triangle Trigonometry:</u>

When a triangle does not have a right angle, it's called an oblique triangle. You cannot use SOH-CAH-TOA and the Pythagorean Theorem anymore because they both require right triangles! Instead, you will use one of two laws depending on the type of oblique triangle given.

Law of Sines: If your triangle is oblique, then $\dfrac{a}{sin\alpha} = \dfrac{b}{sin\beta} = \dfrac{c}{sin\gamma}$.

Note: You must have three out of four pieces of information to start, and the only three types of triangles this will happen with is the SSA, ASA and AAS triangles. The SSS and SAS triangles require the Law of Cosines.

Law of Cosines: If your triangle is oblique, then $a^2 = b^2 + c^2 - 2bccos\alpha$,

$$b^2 = a^2 + c^2 - 2accos\beta \text{ and}$$

$$c^2 = a^2 + b^2 - 2abcos\gamma.$$

Note: You will use Law of Cosines to solve SSS and SAS oblique triangles.

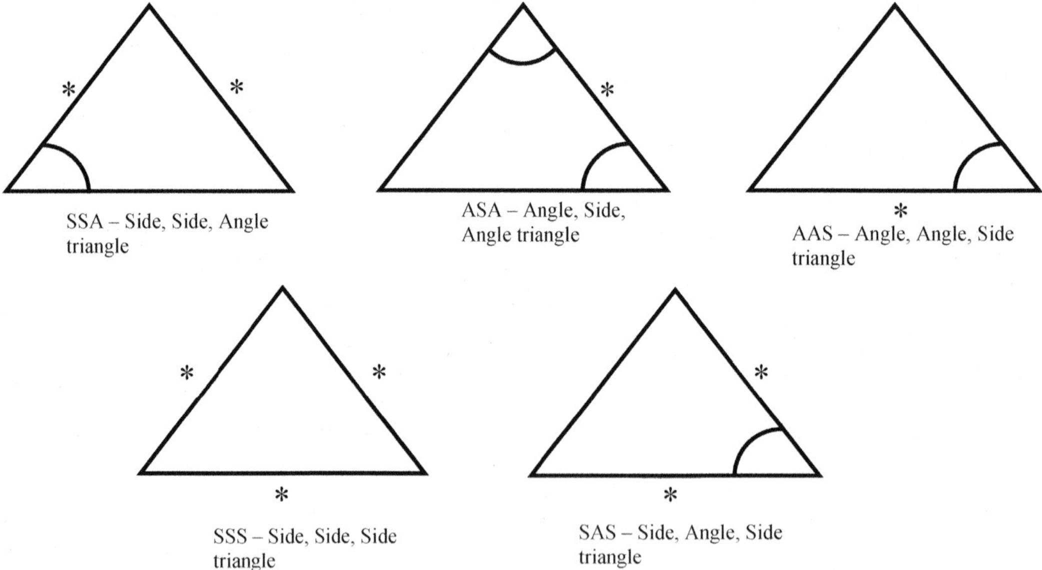

Important Note: For everyone to get the same answer in these oblique triangle problems, it's important to label your triangle so that side "a" is across from α, side "b" is across from angle β and side c is across from angle γ.

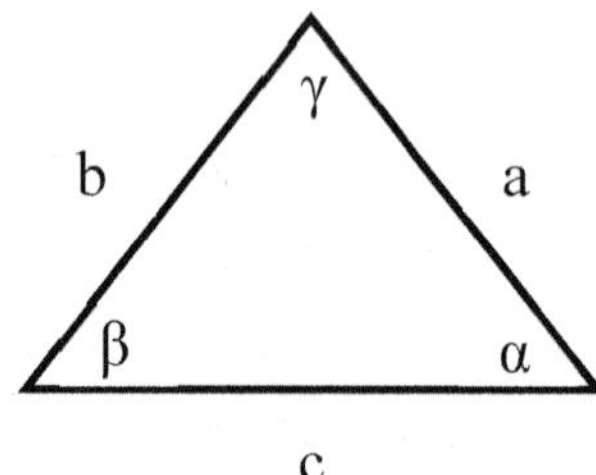

Example 3: Solve an oblique triangle if α=13°, β=38° and b = 17.

Step 1: Draw and label a triangle, making sure to follow the Important Note from above.

Step 2: Identify the type of oblique triangle you are given. In this case, if drawn and labeled correctly, you should have an AAS triangle. This means you should apply the Law of Sines.

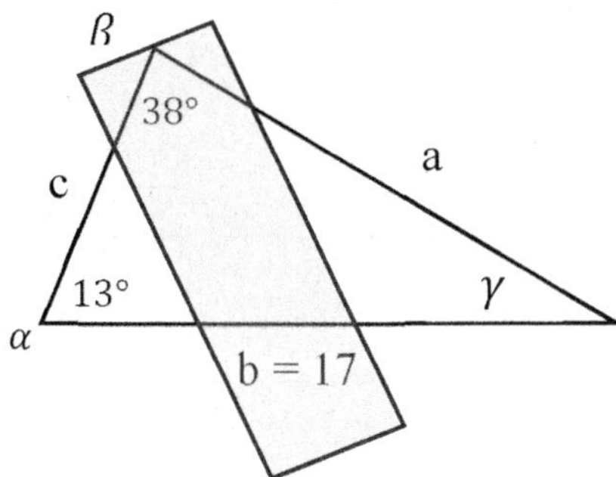

Step 3: Start with the angle and the **corresponding** opposite side that are given, in this case b and β. Write them as a ratio with the side in the numerator.

$$\frac{17}{sin38°}$$

Step 4: The only other value you know is that $\alpha = 13°$, so your other ratio should be:

$$\frac{a}{sin13°}$$

Step 5: Set up a proportion by equating both ratios. $\frac{17}{sin38°} = \frac{a}{sin13°}$

Cross-multiply and solve for your variable "a":

$$17sin13° = a\,sin38°$$

$$\frac{17sin13°}{sin38°} = a$$

$$a \approx 6$$

Step 6: To "solve" a triangle means to find all the missing sides and angles. We can find "c" or γ next. The order doesn't matter. To find γ, recall the three angles of a triangle must sum to 180°.

So, $13° + 38° + \gamma = 180°$ ➔ $\gamma = 129°$.

(Note: You cannot simply use the Pythagorean Theorem since it's not a right triangle!)

Step 7: Now, to find "c", use the Law of Sines again. Always stick with the original angle and side you used that were given. Using a rounded value you calculated could result in error. Set up the proportion and solve through cross multiplication as follows:

$$\frac{17}{sin38*} = \frac{c}{sin\,129°} \;\rightarrow\; 17sin129° = csin38° \;\rightarrow\; c = \frac{17sin129°}{sin38°} \approx 21.$$

The best way to ensure your answers "seem" right is to (1) make sure all the angles add up to 180° and (2) make sure the largest angle corresponds to the largest side and the smallest angle corresponds to the smallest side. If these two conditions are not met, you have one or more errors.

Example 4: Suzie walks from her campsite at a bearing of $N16°E$ at a pace of 30 meters per minute. Mary walks from the same campsite at a bearing of $N43°W$ at a pace of 42 meters per minute. Six minutes later, what is the distance between Suzie and Mary?

Step 1: Recall that to draw a bearing, the angle must be drawn relative to the N-S line (or y-axis)

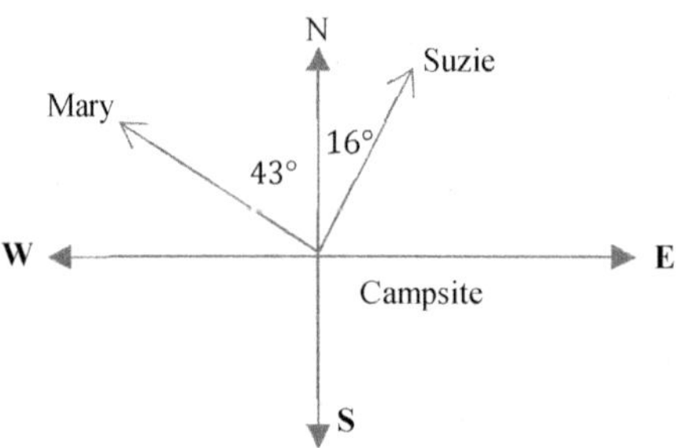

Step 2: Calculate the distances by using the formula distance = rate x time (d = rt) for each person.

$$\text{Suzie: } 30\,\frac{m}{min} \, x \; 6min = 180m \quad \text{and Mary: } 42\,\frac{m}{min} \, x \; 6min = 252\,m$$

Step 3: Determine the type of triangle and determine the method.

Step 4: Using the Law of Cosines, you can write:

$$x^2 = (180)^2 + (252)^2 - 2(180)(252)cos59°$$

$$x = \pm\sqrt{32,400 + 63,504 - 90,720cos59°} \approx 222m.$$

Since it's a distance, the answer should be positive.

Areas of Oblique Triangles

The area of an oblique triangle can be found using one of these formulas: $A = \frac{1}{2}absin\gamma$ or $A = \frac{1}{2}bcsin\alpha$ or $A = \frac{1}{2}acsin\beta$, depending on which values you know about the triangle.

If given an SSS triangle without an angle, you can use Heron's Formula, which says

$$A = \sqrt{s(s-a)(s-b)(s-c)} \text{ where } s = \frac{1}{2}(a+b+c).$$

Example 5: Using the given information in Example 4 only, find the area of the triangle. Then, use all three sides and recalculate the area using Heron's Formula. Can you explain why the answers differ?

Step 1: Label your triangle with a, b and c and also the corresponding angle opposite the side. It doesn't matter which label you use so long as "a" is across from α, "b" is across from β and "c" is across from γ.

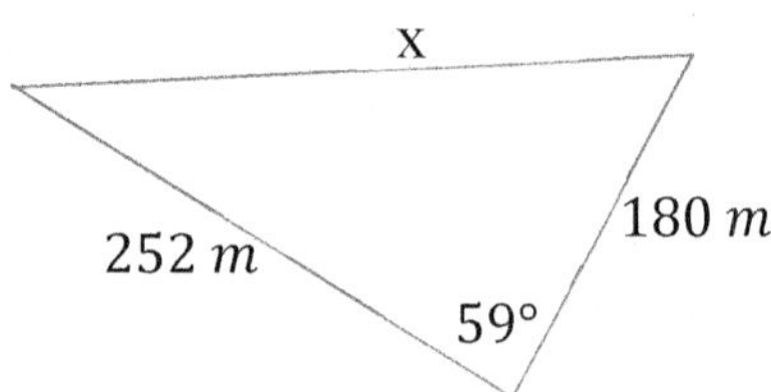

Step 2: Use the formula $A = \frac{1}{2}absin\gamma$ since you know a, b and γ.

Thus, $A = \frac{1}{2}(180)(252)sin59° \approx 19{,}441ft^2$.

Step 3: Using the sides a = 180, b = 252 and c = 222 (from Example 4), apply Heron's formula.

$$s = \frac{1}{2}(180 + 252 + 222) = 327 \text{ and } A =$$
$$\sqrt{327(327 - 180)(327 - 252)(327 - 222)} \approx 19{,}456ft^2.$$

The reason the two answers differ is because this example is using the "222" value from Example 4, which was rounded. When using a rounded value in another calculation, this is called "rounding error". To avoid this, you would have to use the unrounded value stored in your calculator from Example 4 for this example instead of typing in the "222".

Section 10: Vectors

<u>Definitions and Notation</u>

A **scalar** is a quantity without a direction. Some examples are time, temperature and volume.

A **vector** (also called a "directed line segment") is a quantity with a direction. Some examples are velocity, force, acceleration and work.

Notations:

- **Component form:** The vector from $(0, 0)$ to a point $(a_1 a_2)$ is the vector $\mathbf{a} = <a_1, a_2>$.

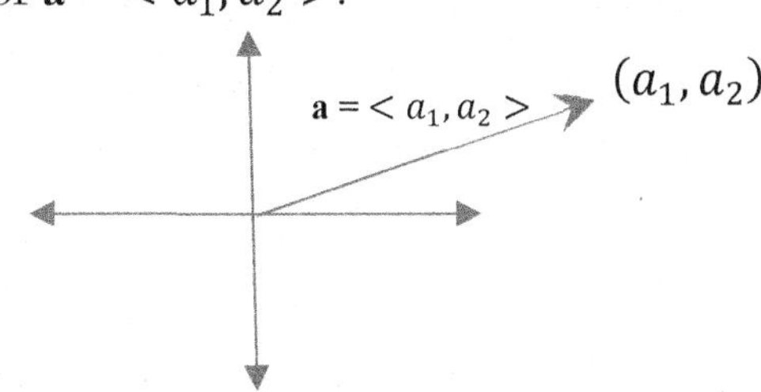

- **i,j – form:** Recall the **i** vector is a horizontal unit vector from $(0,0)$ to $(1,0)$ and the **j** vector is a vertical unit vector from $(0, 0)$ to $(0, 1)$. Then, the i,j-form of the vector would be: $\mathbf{a} = a_1\boldsymbol{i} + a_2\boldsymbol{j}$. Sometimes, this is referred to as a "linear combination in **i** and **j**".

- Combining the two, $\mathbf{a} = <a_1, a_2> = a_1\boldsymbol{i} + a_2\boldsymbol{j}$.

- The magnitude of a vector (its quantity) is derived from the Pythagorean Theorem as: $\|\boldsymbol{a}\| = \sqrt{(a_1)^2 + (a_2)^2}$.

Note: When vectors are written in component or i,j-form, they always start at the $(0, 0)$.

Example 1: Plot the vectors $\mathbf{a} = <-3, 1>$ and $\mathbf{s} = 4\mathbf{i} - 2\mathbf{j}$. Find the magnitudes of each.

Solution: When plotting vectors in either component or **i,j**-form, always start at $(0,0)$ and draw a vector to the ordered pair (a_1, a_2).

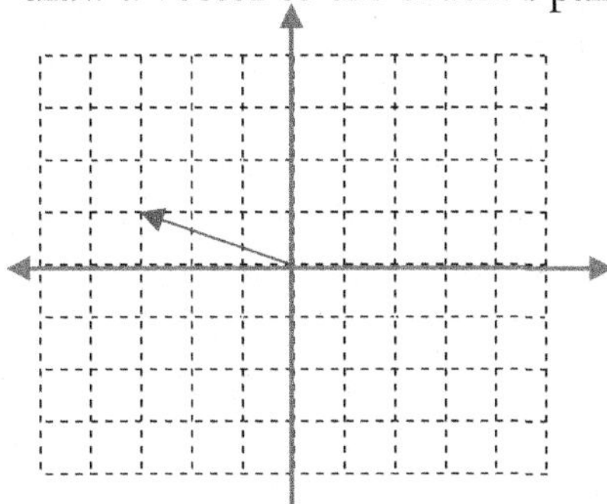
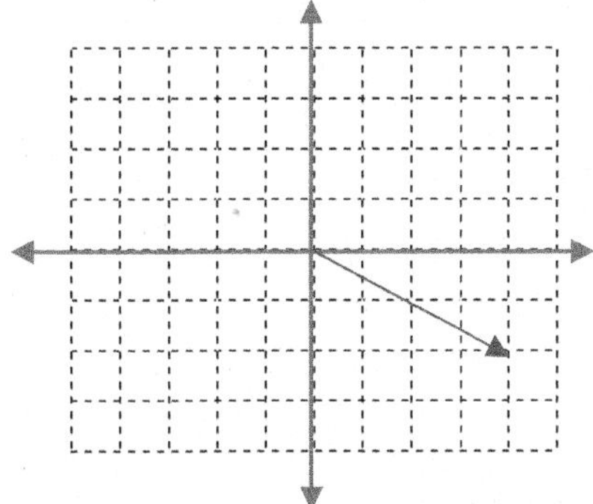

The magnitudes are:

$$\|\mathbf{a}\| = \sqrt{(-3)^2 + (1)^2} = \sqrt{10} \approx 3.2$$

and

$$\|\mathbf{s}\| = \sqrt{(4)^2 + (-2)^2} = \sqrt{20} \approx 4.5.$$

Note: If you make perpendicular lines from each vector's terminal point to the x-axis to form right triangles, you can see the magnitude of a vector is simply the hypotenuse, which is why the magnitude formula is really just the Pythagorean Theorem in disguise!

<u>Operations on Vectors</u>

Scalar multiplication: If you multiply a vector with a real number, that number will make the vector grow or shrink or stay the same. If the number is negative, it will change the direction of the vector.

In other words, if k is a real number and **v** is a vector, then kv is a scalar multiple of **v** and the new vector $kv = k < v_1, v_2 >=< kv_1, kv_2 >$ or $kv = k(v_1 \boldsymbol{i} + v_2 \boldsymbol{j}) = kv_1 \boldsymbol{i} + kv_2 \boldsymbol{j}$

Adding two vectors:

The sum of two vectors **a** and **b** is $\boldsymbol{a} + \boldsymbol{b} =< a_1, a_2 > +< b_1, b_2 >=< a_1 + b_1, a_2 + b_2 >$ or

$$\boldsymbol{a} + \boldsymbol{b} = (a_1 \boldsymbol{i} + a_2 \boldsymbol{j}) + (b_1 \boldsymbol{i} + b_2 \boldsymbol{j}) = (a_1 + a_2)\boldsymbol{i} + (b_1 + b_2)\boldsymbol{j}.$$

Subtracting two vectors:

The difference of two vectors **a** and **b** is $\boldsymbol{a} - \boldsymbol{b} =< a_1, a_2 > -< b_1, b_2 >=< a_1 - b_1, a_2 - b_2 >$ or

$$\boldsymbol{a} - \boldsymbol{b} = (a_1 \boldsymbol{i} - a_2 \boldsymbol{j}) + (b_1 \boldsymbol{i} - b_2 \boldsymbol{j}) = (a_1 - a_2)\boldsymbol{i} + (b_1 - b_2)\boldsymbol{j}.$$

Example 2: Given a vector **v** below, draw the vectors 3v, -v and $-1.5v$. Then, draw the vector **a** = <-3, -1>. Find and plot the vectors 2a and -3a.

Solution: To draw a vector 3**v,** you will draw a vector anywhere on the page that is in the same direction as vector **v** but three times as long.

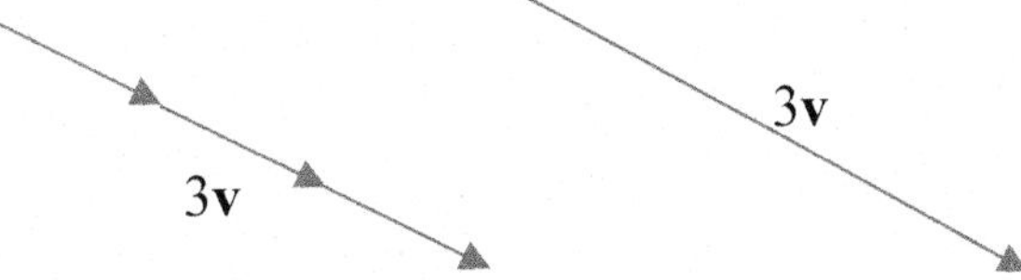

To draw the vector -**v**, draw a vector anywhere on the page that is the same length as **v** but in the exact opposite direction.

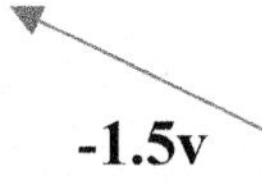

When drawing -1.5v, since the coefficient on the vector is negative, it will be in the opposite direction as vector **v**. Since the coefficient is 1.5, it will be one and a half times as long as vector **v**.

The vector **a** = <-3, -1> starts at the origin and points to the ordered pair (3, -1).

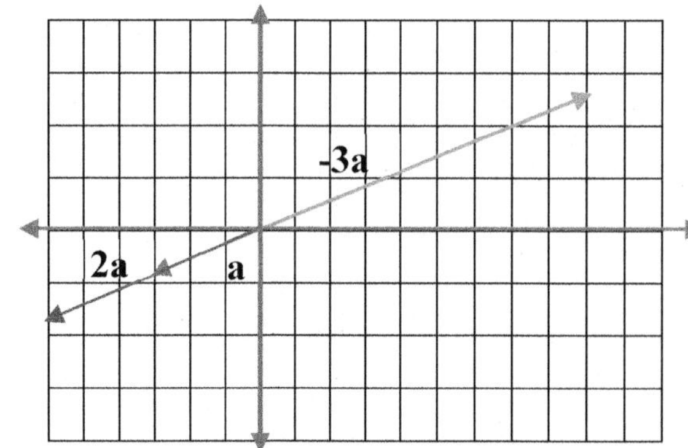

$2\mathbf{a} = 2<-3, -1> = <(2)(-3), (2)(-1)> = <-6, -2>$

$-3\mathbf{a} = -3<-3, -1> = <9, 3>$

Example 3: Given vector **s** = 3**i** – **j** and **t** = 4**i** + 2**j**, find a) **t+s**, b) **s-t**, c) 2**t** – 5**s**.

a)   **t** + **s** = (4**i**+2**j**) + (3**i** – **j**) = (4 + 3)**i** + (2 – 1)**j** = 7**i** + **j**

b)   **s** – **t** = (3**i** – **j**) – (4**i** + 2**j**) = (3-4)**i** + (-1-2)**j** = -**i**-3**j**

c)   2**t** – 5**s** = 2(4**i** + 2**j**) -5 (3**i** – **j**) = (8**i** + 4**j**) + (-15**i** + 5**j**) = -7**i** + 9**j**

<u>The Vector Equation of a Straight Line</u>

If you have a point $P = (p_1, p_2)$ and a vector $\mathbf{v} = \langle v_1, v_2 \rangle$, you can describe the points of the straight line through the point in the direction of the vector with the following formula: $(x,y) = (p_1, p_2) + k(v_1, v_2)$, where k is any real number. (Note that $\langle v_1, v_2 \rangle$ denotes vector but in the formula, you use the ordered pair (v_1, v_2).

Example 4: Write the equation of the line through the point (-2, 1) in the direction of <5, -4>. Then, find three points on the line.

Solution: Using the formula, $(x,y) = (-2, 1) + k(5, -4)$.

Select **any** three values for k.

If k = 0: $(x,y) = (-2, 1) + (0)(5,-4) = (-2, 1) + (0, 0) = (-2, 1)$.

If k = -5: $(x, y) = (-2, 1) + (-5)(5, -4) = (-2, 1) + (-25, 20) = (-27, 21)$

If k = 2: $(x, y) = (-2, 1) + (2)(5, -4) = (-2, 1) + (10, -8) = (9, -7)$.

All of these points are on the same line, specifically the ones that passes through (-2, 1) and is in the direction of (5, -4).

<u>The Ratio Theorem of Vectors</u>

If a point P on a line segment **AB** divides the segment into a ratio of two lengths, this theorem will help to find the coordinates of the point P by finding the vector **p**. If **a** is a vector from the origin to (a_1, a_2), **b** is a vector from the origin to (b_1, b_2) and **p** is a vector from the origin to (p_1, p_2), then $\boldsymbol{p} = \left(\frac{AP}{AP+PB}\right)\boldsymbol{a} + \left(\frac{PB}{AP+PB}\right)\boldsymbol{b}.$

The corresponding point to vector $\mathbf{p} = \;< p_1, p_2 >$ is the point (p_1, p_2).

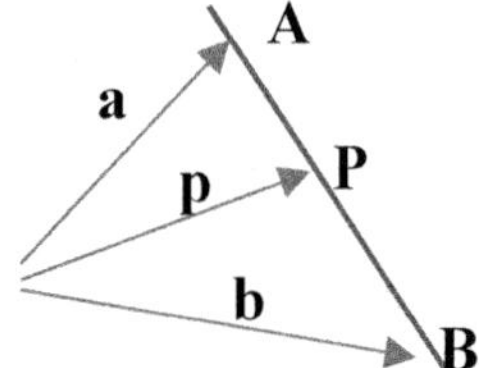

Example 5: If there is a point A = (3, 1) and a point B = (7, 4) and some point P between AB such that that ratio is AP:PB = 2:5, what is the coordinate of the point P?

Solution: Using the formula, $\boldsymbol{p} = \left(\frac{AP}{AP+PB}\right)\boldsymbol{a} + \left(\frac{PB}{AP+PB}\right)\boldsymbol{b}$

$$= \left(\frac{2}{2+5}\right) < 3,1 > + \left(\frac{5}{2+5}\right) < 7,4 >$$

$$= \left(\frac{2}{7}\right) < 3,1 > + \left(\frac{5}{7}\right) < 7,4 >$$

$$=< \frac{6}{7}, \frac{2}{7} > +< \frac{35}{7}, \frac{20}{7} >$$

$$=< \frac{41}{7}, \frac{22}{7} >$$

Therefore, the point P will be $\left(\frac{41}{7}, \frac{22}{7}\right).$

Section 11: Box Plots

Box Plot Basics

A **box plot** (a.k.a. **box and whisker plot**) is a type of graph that displays the five-number summary of a set of data. The plot show the minimum, the first quartile, the median, the third quartile and the maximum.

- **Recall**: the **median** of a set of numbers is the halfway point between the set of numbers listed in order.
- **Recall**: the **first quartile** is the halfway point between the minimum and the median.
- **Recall**: the third quartile is the halfway point between the median and the maximum.

-A box plot looks like this:

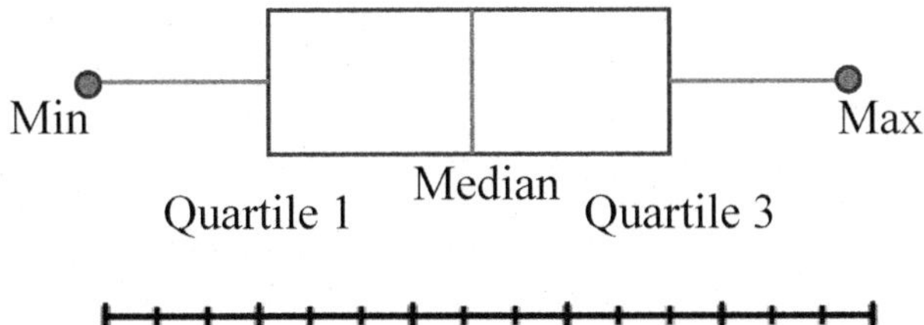

Example 1: There are ten gems that have the following weights in grams:

$$23, 14, 17, 25, 16, 19, 27, 16, 25 , 28$$

Create a box plot of the data.

Solution:

Step 1: Always arrange your data in ascending order.

$$14, 16, 16, 17, 19, 23, 25, 25, 27, 28.$$

Step 2: Now, find the median by locating the middle of your data and then finding the average of the two numbers adjacent to the middle.

$$14, 16, 16, 17, 19 \mid 23, 25, 25, 27, 28$$

Median: $\dfrac{19+23}{2} = \dfrac{42}{2} = 21$

Step 3: To find the first quartile, take the average of the minimum of 14 and the median of 21.

First quartile: $\dfrac{14+21}{2} = \dfrac{35}{2} = 17.5$

Step 4: To find the third quartile, take the average of the median of 21 and the maximum of 28.

$$\text{Third quartile: } \frac{21+28}{2} = \frac{49}{2} = 24.5$$

Step 5: List the five-number summary.

14, 17.5, 21, 24.5, 28

Step 6: Draw vertical lines atop a number line at the 17.5, 21 and 24.5 points and connect in a box. Draw a whisker to the left to the minimum at 14. Draw a whisker to the right to the maximum at 28.

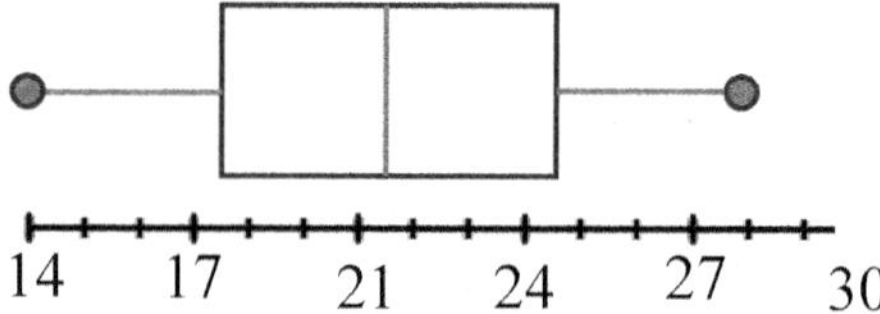

Interpreting Quartiles

The five-number summary of a box plot divides the set of data into sections that each contain approximately 25% of the data in that set.

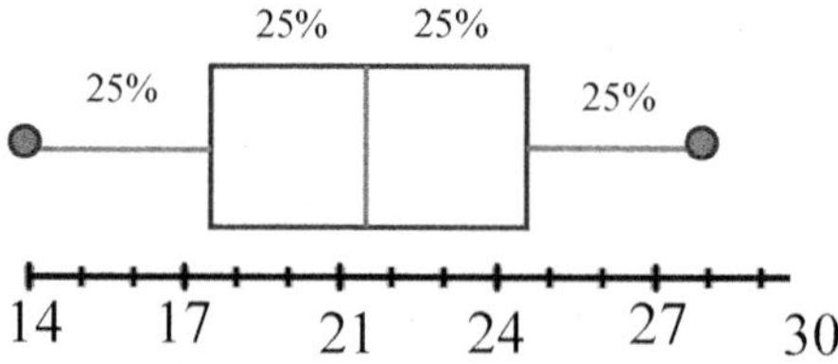

Example 2: Referring to the box plot above, about what percent of the gems have a weight less than 24.5 grams?

Solution: Jf you locate 24.5 grams on the box plot, you see it's at the third quartile. That means each quartile before it has 25% of the gems. Adding them up, you will get that 75% of the gems that weigh less than 24.5 grams.

Example 3: Two different sections of a Statistics class took Test #1 and these box plots represent how they did.

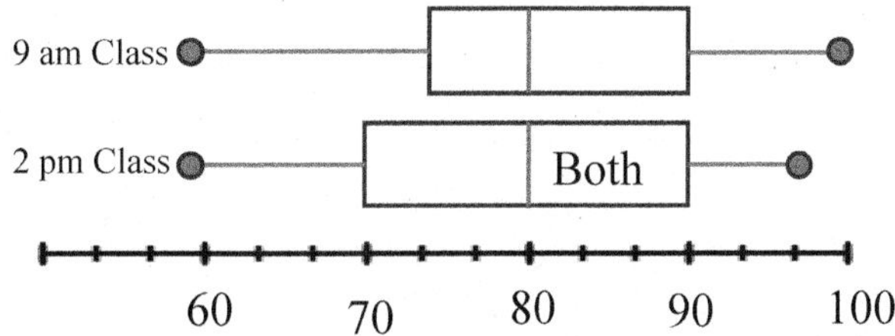

What do these box plots show about how the 9 am class did compared to the 2 pm class?

Solution:

You can see that both classes had the same lowest score of 60%.

The 9 am class had a higher maximum score than the 2 pm class.

Both classes had the same median score of 80%. So, half the class did worse than 80% and half the class did better for both sections.

In the 9 am class, 25% of the students got between 60% and 74%, 25% of the students scored between 74% and 80%, another 25% scored between 80% and 90% and the last quarter scored between 90% and 100%.

In the 2 pm class, 25% of the students got between 60% and 70%, another quarter of the students scored between 70% and 80%, a third quarter scored between 80% and 90% and the last quarter between 90% and approximately 97%.

Outliers in a Box and Whiskers Plot

An **outlier** is a value that noticeably deviates from the other members of a sample to which it belongs.

To determine if a value is considered an outlier, you must find if it falls outside a particular range. To calculate the lower and upper bounds of the range, do the following:

Step 1: Find the IQR (inter-quartile range), the distance between the first and third quartiles.

Step 2: Multiply the IQR by 1.5.

Step 3: Subtract the value you just found in Step 2 from the 1st Quartile to get your lower bound.

Step 4: Add the value you just found in Step 2 to the 3rd Quartile to get your upper bound.

Any value that falls outside the range of values determined by the lower and upper bounds are called **outliers.**

Example 4: For the data set 1 , 3, 4, 5, 5, 11, 12, 13, 14, 19, find the five-number summary and the outlier range. Are any of the values in the set considered an outlier?

Step 1: Find the five-number summary for the data, which is already in order.

Min: 1

Max: 19

Median: $(5 + 11) / 2 = 8$

1st Quartile: 4

3rd Quartile: 13

Step 2: Find the IQR by subtracting the 1st Quartile value from the 3rd Quartile value.

$13 - 4 = 9$

Step 3: Multiply the IQR by 1.5.

$9 \times 1.5 = 13.5$

Step 4: Subtract 13.5 from the 1st Quartile.

$4 - 13.5 = -9.5.$

Step 5: Add 13.5 to the 3rd Quartile.

$13 + 13.5 = 26.5.$

The range for outliers is -9.5 to 26.5, so any value in the data set lower than -9.5 or above 26.5 would be considered an outlier. None of the data in this set are below or above the bounds, so there are no outliers.

Section 13: Cumulative Frequencies

<u>Cumulative Frequencies Basics</u>
- A **frequency** of a value in a data set is how many times it occurs.

- A **cumulative frequency** is often referred to as a "running total" of the frequencies for which each data is represented. When you add up each previous frequency, you are accumulating frequencies into a total or sum.

- **Cumulative frequency graphs / curves** are graphs of the item being measured in the data set versus the cumulative frequency values. These graphs are helpful for finding out about the popularity of a certain type of data or about the likelihood a given value will fall within a certain frequency distribution.

Example 1: Each month, you record the number of times you stayed up all night studying for an exam. Find the cumulative frequency for each month.

Month	Frequency
September	5
October	7
November	4
December	2
January	3
February	6
March	5
April	4
May	7
June	2

Solution: To find a cumulative frequency, take the first value of 5 and then add the next value to it. This means in October, you have studied a total of 12 nights. For the next month, November, add the frequency to your running total of 12 to get 16. Proceed in that manner until you get to the last month listed. That should match the total of all the frequencies in your frequencies column.

Month	Frequency	Cumulative Frequency
September	5	➔ Start with 5.
October	7	5 + 7 = 12
November	4	12 + 4 = 16
December	2	16 + 2 = 18
January	3	18 + 3 = 21
February	6	21 + 6 = 27
March	5	27 + 5 = 32
April	4	32 + 4 = 36
May	7	36 + 7 = 43
June	2	43 + 2 = 45

To check your work, add up the values in the frequency column: $5 + 7 + 4 + 2 + 3 + 6 + 5 + 4 + 7 + 2 = 45$.

Example 2: For the data below, which represents how many movie tickets were purchased by people of certain ages, plot a cumulative frequency curve.

Age	Frequency
11	100
12	93
13	127
14	150
15	178
16	198

Solution: Calculate the cumulative frequency values as you did in Example 1. In a cumulative frequency curve (also called an "ogive"), always plot the cumulative frequency values on your y-axis. Plot "age" on your x-axis. Pick an appropriate scale for each and label each axis.

Age	Frequency	Cumulative Frequency
11	100	100
12	93	100+93 = 193
13	127	193 + 127 = 320
14	150	320 + 150 = 470
15	178	470 + 178 = 648
16	198	648 + 198 = 846

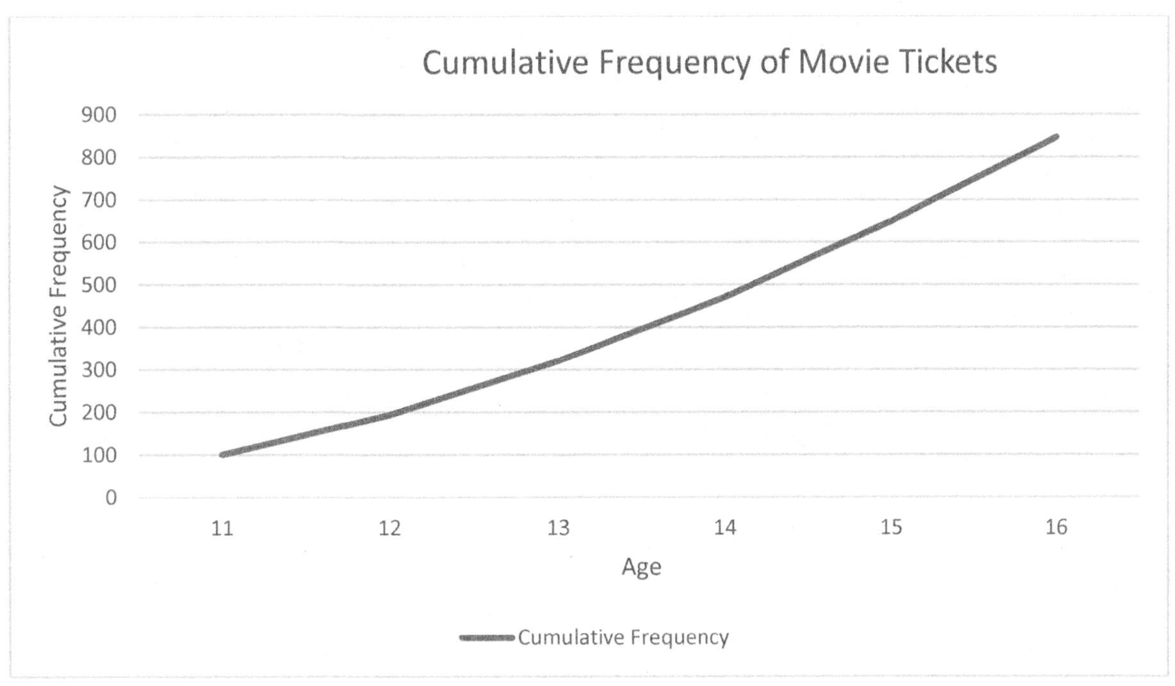

Percentiles

A **percentile** is a percentage of a data set. Percentiles are used to understand how many of a given set of values will fall within a specific percentage range.

For example, if you are told your SAT score is in the 95th percentile, that means that 95% of the scores were below yours. This does not mean necessarily that your score was a 95%, however. In other words, out of 100 test takers, 95 did worse than you. You could have scored a 20%, but if everyone else except 5% got less than 20%, you would still be in the 95th percentile.

To calculate a percentile, use the formula:

$$P_m = \frac{m}{100} \times N$$

where P_m is the percentile and m represents the specific percentile you're finding and N is the total number of elements in your data set.

Example 3: Find the 70th percentile in the set of fifteen test scores shown below.

48, 72, 51, 98, 86, 90, 82, 66, 61, 70, 58, 69, 76, 94, 31

Solution: Since the percentile is 70, let m = 70. There are fifteen values in the data set, so N = 15. Now, $P_{70} = \frac{70}{100} x15 = 10.5$. Round up to the nearest whole number to get a 70th percentile of 11. Now, put the data in order from smallest to largest value and count the eleventh number from the left.

31, 48, 51, 58, 61, 66, 69, 79, 72, 76, 82, 86, 90, 94, 98

This means that 70% of the scores were below 82 in this set of data.

Medians and Interquartile Ranges

The **25th percentile** is also called the **1st Quartile.**

The **50th percentile** is also called the **2nd Quartile** or **median.**

The **75th percentile** is also called the **3rd Quartile.**

The **interquartile range (IQR)** is the **3rd Quartile less the 1st Quartile.** So, **IQR = Q3 − Q1**. This shows where 50% of your scores fall. It focuses on the middle instead of extreme higher or lower scores.

Example 4: For the following set of data, find the three quartiles and the interquartile range.,

21, 4, 38, 27, 14, 13, 1, 29, 31, 33, 8, 11, 35, 20, 25

Solution:

Step 1: Put the data in order from lowest to highest.

1, 4, 8, 11, 13, 14, 20, 21, 25, 27, 29, 31, 33, 35, 38

This is the median.

> **Note:** If you used the formula $P_{50} = \frac{50}{100}x15 = 7.5$. Round up to the nearest whole number of 8 and count 8 numbers from the left. When you do, you also get 21.

Step 3: To find the Q1 value, find the median of the left side of the data set to get 11.

> **Note:** With the formula, you get $P_{25} = \frac{25}{100}x15 = 3.75$. Round up to 4 and count 4 values from the left to also get 11.

Step 4: The Q3 value is the median of the right side of the data set. Count from the median of 21 to the end and find the exact middle to be 31. With the formula, you get $P_{75} = \dfrac{75}{100} x15 = 11.25$. Round up to 12 and count 12 values from the left to get a 31 also.

Step 5: Find the IQR by subtracting Q3 – Q1: 31 – 11 = 20. So, half the data in the set is between 11 and 31, a range of 20 values.

Example 5: For the data below, which represents heights of students under 170cm in a Statistics class, calculate the cumulative frequencies, construct a cumulative frequency curve and then calculate and label the median, Quartile 1, Quartile 3 and the interquartile range.

Height	Frequency
152	2
154	4
156	6
f158	3
160	10
162	7
164	8
166	7
168	6
170	3

Solution:

Height	Frequency	Cumulative Frequency
152	2	2
154	4	6
156	6	12
158	3	15
160	10	25
162	7	32
164	8	40
166	7	47
168	6	53
170	3	56

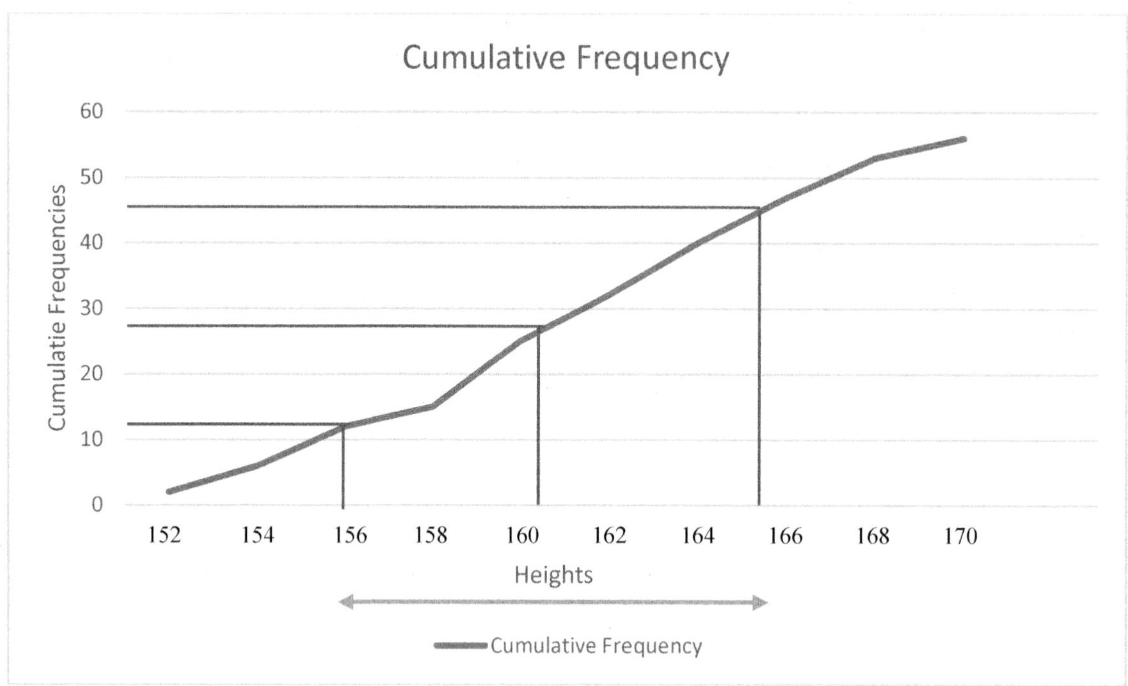

The median falls between the 25 and the 32, so find the average: (25 + 32) / 2 = 28.5.

The Q1 value is the median of the left side of the data set, so you should get 12.

The Q3 value is the median of the right side of the data set, so you should get 47.

The IQR is 47 – 12 = 35, meaning half the cumulative frequencies are between 12 and 47.

Notice where the green arrow indicates the IQR that 50% of the heights fall between 156cm and almost 166cm of those in the Statistics class whose heights were below 170cm.

Section 14: Histograms

<u>Histograms Basics</u>

A **histogram** is a bar graph that shows the frequency distribution / shape of a set of a data that has been divided into **classes** or **bins**.

The major difference is that a histogram is only used to plot the frequency of score occurrences in a continuous data set that has been divided into classes. Bar charts more generally can be used for other types of variables and to describe a wider variety of data sets.

Example 1: Sort the ages below into groups starting with 12 years up through 31 years and counting by fours. Record how many values fall into each group. Then, make a histogram of the data.

13, 24, 15, 23, 30, 28, 27, 27, 26, 25, 17, 17, 18, 20, 24, 12, 16

Solution:

Sort the data in order: 12, 13, 15, 16, 17, 17, 18, 20, 23, 24, 24, 25, 26, 27, 27, 28, 30

Age Range	Frequency
12 – 15	3
16 – 19	4
20 – 23	2
24 – 27	6
28 - 31	2

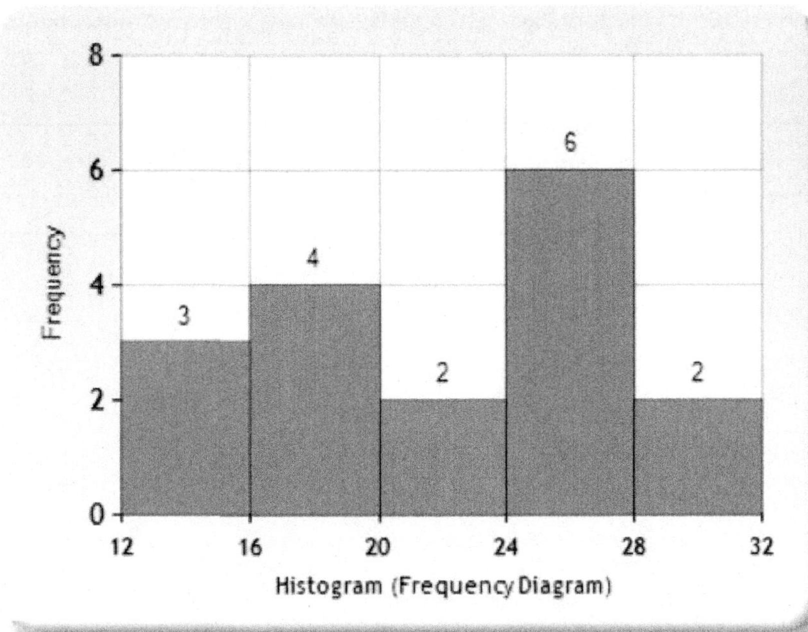

<u>Frequency Density</u>

A **frequency density** is the frequency value divided by the class width.

$$frequency\ density = \frac{frequency}{class\ width}$$

You can also solve for frequency in the equation and find another equivalence:

$$frequency = frequency\ density \times class\ width$$

Note: The class widths do not have to be the same for each class!

Example 2: For the set of data below, which represents the number of people in each age category who attended the baseball game last Saturday, find the frequency densities and then graph the attendees versus the frequency densities.

Age Range	Frequency
10 – 15	56
15 – 24	28
25 – 40	33
41 – 55	22
56 - 80	14

Solution:

Make sure to count the class width carefully for each. Then, divide the frequency by the class width for each to find the frequency density.

Age Range	Frequency	Class Width	Frequency Density
10 – 15	56	6	$56 \div 6 \approx 9.3$
16 – 24	28	9	$28 \div 9 \approx 3.1$
25 – 40	33	16	$33 \div 16 \approx 2.1$
41 – 55	22	15	$22 \div 15 \approx 1.5$
56 - 80	14	25	$14 \div 25 \approx 0.6$

Plot the graph with the age group versus the frequency densities.

Note: The graph below shows the age groups as if they're the same width, which is not true. This is sometimes done, but a better graph would show each width relative to the others so you could compare the sizes of widths with the density.

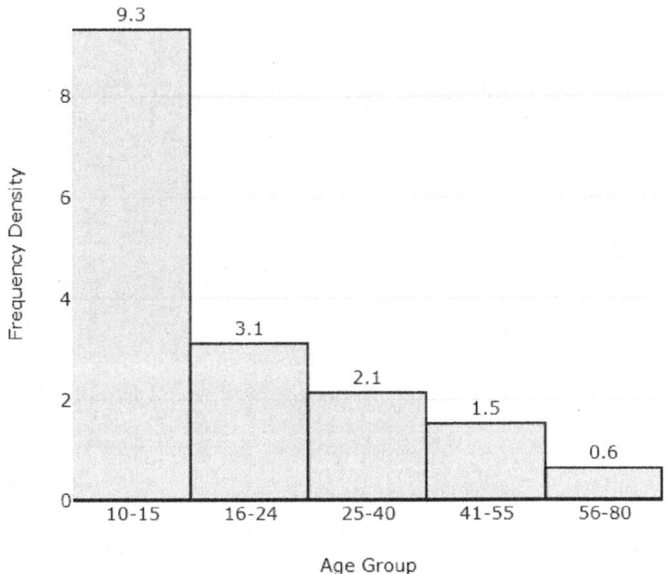

Example 3: Using the histogram below to find the frequencies of each height group.

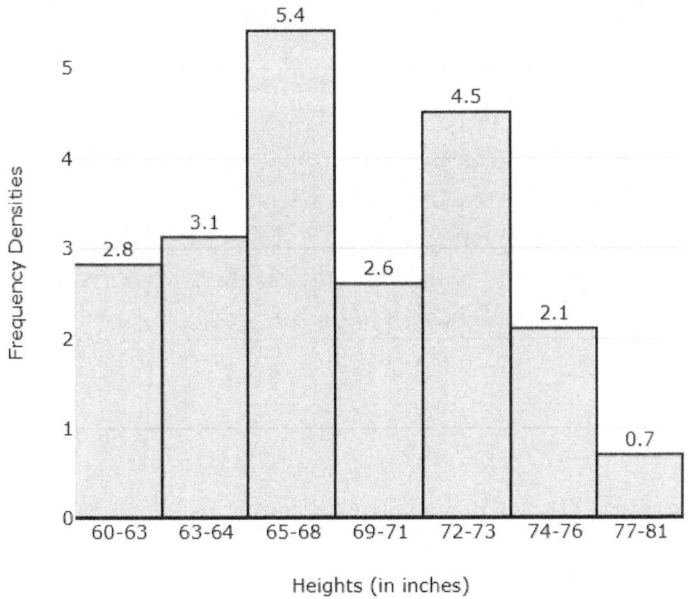

 Recall that the frequency is the frequency density multiplied by the class width.

Frequency Density	Class Width	Frequency
2.8	4	2.8 x 4 = 11.2
3.1	2	3.1 x 2 = 6.2
5.4	4	5.4 x 4 = 21.6
2.6	3	2.6 x 3 = 7.8
4.5	2	4.5 x 2 = 9
2.1	3	2.1 x 3 = 6.3
0.7	5	0.7 x 5 = 3.5

Example 4: For the data in the graph in Example 3, answer questions about the graph.

a) What is the most popular height group of those in the data set?
b) What is the least dense height group? What does that mean?
c) Could you reorganize the graph into equal height classes? Why or why not?
d) If there was a category of $81 - 87$ that had fifteen people within those heights, what would the density be? Would it be less or more dense if the class width was $81 - 85$?

Solution:

a) In the graph, the most dense height group with the highest bar at 5.4 is the $65 - 68$ inches height group. With the frequency calculation, you can see the highest frequency was in that same height group, 21.6 being the largest frequency calculated.
b) The least dense is the $77 - 81$ inch height group, with the lowest bar, the frequency density only a 0.7 and the frequency calculated only a 3.5. This means that the least people sampled fell into this height group.
c) You would not be able to reorganize the graph unless you had the raw data to work with or a distribution into those different height classes given in the problem. There is not enough information to redo the graph.
d) For an $81 - 87$ inch height group, the class width is 7 and the frequency is 15, so $15 / 7 = 2.1$ (approx.) would be the frequency density. If the class width was 5, the frequency density would be $15 / 5 = 3$, meaning the height category would be more dense if the width was less and less dense for a greater width.

Section 15: Other Graphs

Scatterplots

A scatterplot is a graph of points (x, y) that shows the relationship between two sets of data. Generally, when one plots one of these graphs, they are hoping to find a **trend** in the data which would predictions about the data's behavior.

Example 1: For the lemonade sales versus temperature, where temperature is the x-axis, create a scatterplot of the data. Does the data seem to have a particular trend? If so, what does the trend mean?

Temperature (°F)	Lemonade Sales ($)
70	100
72	103
75	120
77	129
80	132
85	143
90	165
92	165
95	166
100	180

Solution: Make an appropriate scale for the x-axis and the y-axis. Recall that you do not have to start counting at 0 and can make a graph break symbol to start at a higher number. Plot each point and then see if the points seem to form a particular shape.

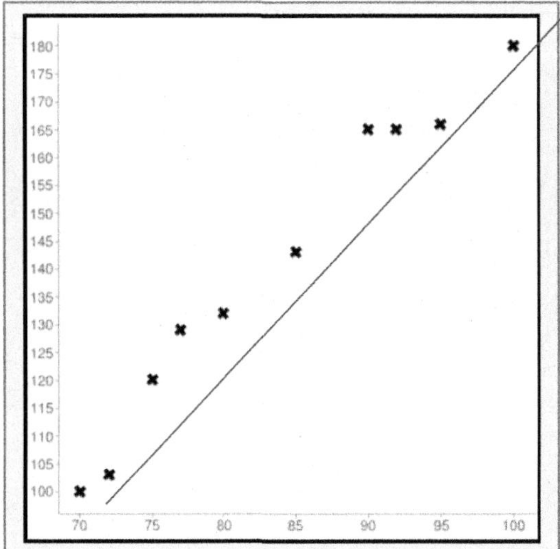

You can see the points trend toward a line, sometimes called the "line of best fit" or "trend line". From this data trend, you can observe that warmer weather tends to lead to increased sales in lemonade.

<u>Line Graphs</u>

A line graph is a bar graph where the centers of each bar top are connected with lines and then the bars are removed. This type of graph is used to emphasize the change from one bar to the next, especially emphasizing transition over time.

Example 2: A bar graph representing the relationship between months and number of hits (in millions) on a popular website is shown below. Find the corresponding line graph.

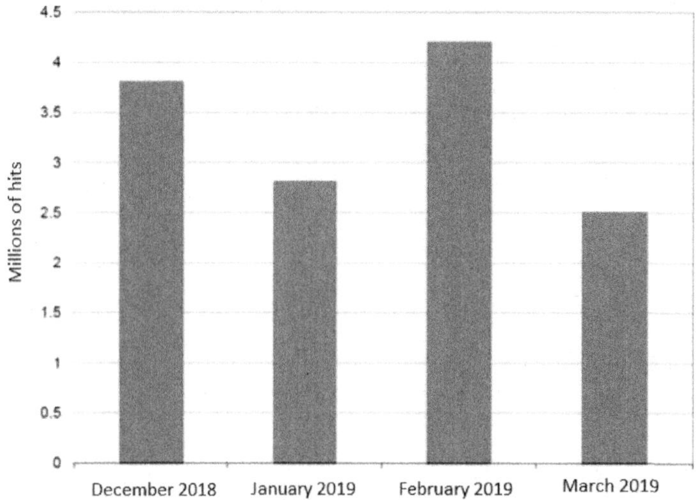

Solution: Find the top center of each bar on the bar graph and connect with a straight line. Then, erase the bars.

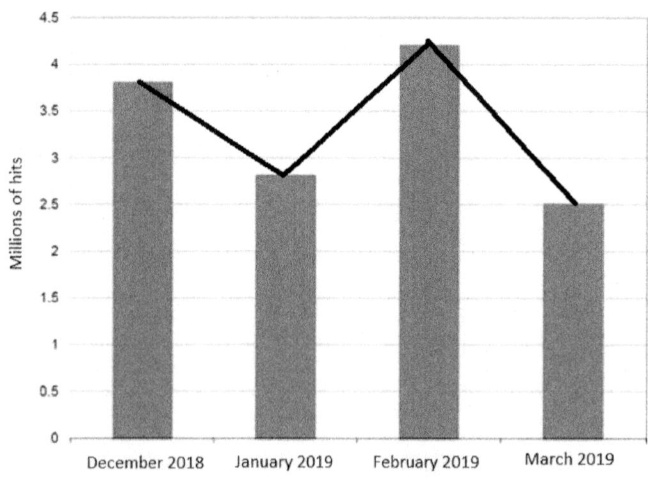

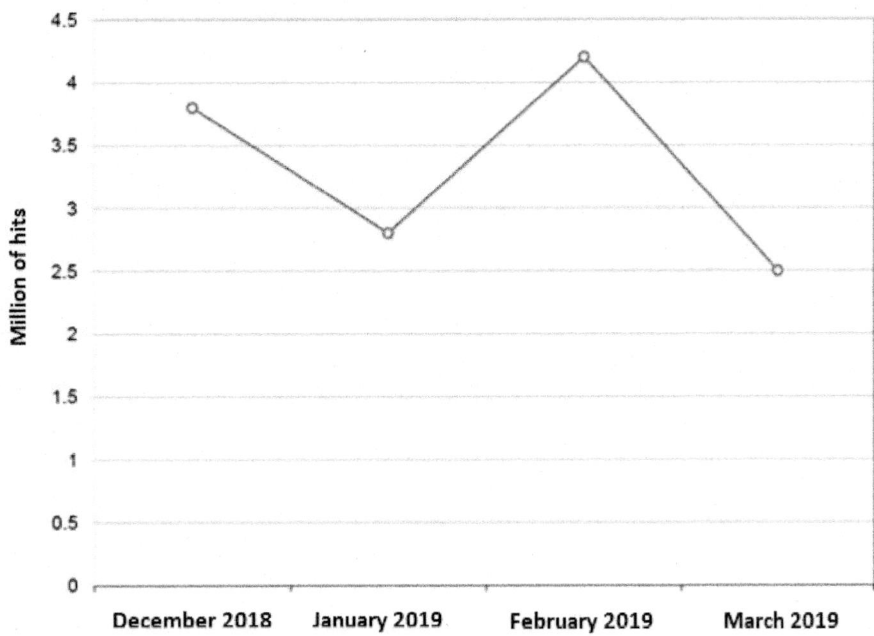

You can much more easily focus on the change from each data maximum when the bars are removed.

Stem-and-Leaf Plot

A stem-and-leaf plot is a special type of table or graph where each value in a set of data is split into a **stem** (the left digit or digits) and a **leaf** (the very right digit or digits). The purpose of this is to show the frequency of some value within another category. Usually, it shows which ones belong to each tens unit, but not always, as shown in the next two examples. In general, these plots show the distribution of the data and its shape.

Example 3: For the data shown below, construct a stem-and-leaf plot.

12, 25, 62, 71, 34, 36, 41, 17, 32, 29, 20, 48, 49, 4, 9, 19, 19, 26

Solution:

Stem	Leaf
0	4 9
1	2 7 9 9
2	0 5 6 9
3	2 4 6
4	1 8 9
5	
6	2
7	1

Example 4: The long-jump distances (in meters) were recorded for a gym class as shown below. Create a stem-and-leaf plot of the data.

2.1, 2.4, 2.4, 2.7. 2.9, 3.2, 3.5, 3.5, 3.5, 3.9, 4.5, 5.0, 5.0

Solution:

Stem	Leaf
2	1 4 4 7 9
3	2 5 5 5 9
4	5
5	0 0

Notice here, you are splitting over the decimal and seeing which tenth belongs to which ones, whereas in Example 3, you are seeing which ones values belong to which tens value.

Pie Charts

A pie chart is a circle divided up to show sizes of sub-groups of data relative to each other. All values in a pie chart should sum to whatever the given total is. If the data is given in percentages, the total should always be 100%.

Example 4: A student appropriated the time in her day according to the schedule below. Find the percentage out of 24 hours that she spends doing each activity and then make a pie-chart to represent her daily tasks.

Time	Activity
7:00 – 8:00 AM	Get ready for school
8:00 AM – 12:00 PM	Attend school
12:00 – 12:45 PM	Eat lunch
12:45 – 3:30 PM	Attend school
3:30 – 7:00 PM	Volunteer time
7:00 – 8:00 PM	Eat dinner / family time
8:00 – 10:00 PM	Homework time
10:00 – 11:30 PM	Online social time

 Figure out the percentage of time the student spent on each out of 24 hours in a day by using the calculation $\frac{time\ spent\ on\ activity\ (in\ hours)}{24\ hours} \times 100\%$.

Time	Activity
12:00 AM – 7:00 AM	Sleep
7:00 – 8:00 AM	Get ready for school
8:00 AM – 12:00 PM	Attend school
12:00 – 12:45 PM	Eat lunch
12:45 – 3:30 PM	Attend school
3:30 – 7:00 PM	Volunteer time
7:00 – 8:00 PM	Eat dinner / family time
8:00 – 10:00 PM	Homework time
10:00 – 11:30 PM	Online social time
11:30 PM – 12:00 AM	Sleep

Activity	Total Time (in hours)	Percentage
Sleep	7.5	(7.5/24)*100=31.25%
Get ready for school	1	(1/24)*100=4.17%
Attend school	6.75	(6.75/24)*100=28.13%
Eat a meal / socialize	1.75	(1.75/24)*100=7.29%
Volunteer time	3.5	(3.5/24)*100= 14.58%
Homework time	2	(2/24)*100= 8.33%

Divide up a circle with these approximated amounts to compare the relative sizes. This type of graph gives a quick visual comparison of time the student spent on each activity.

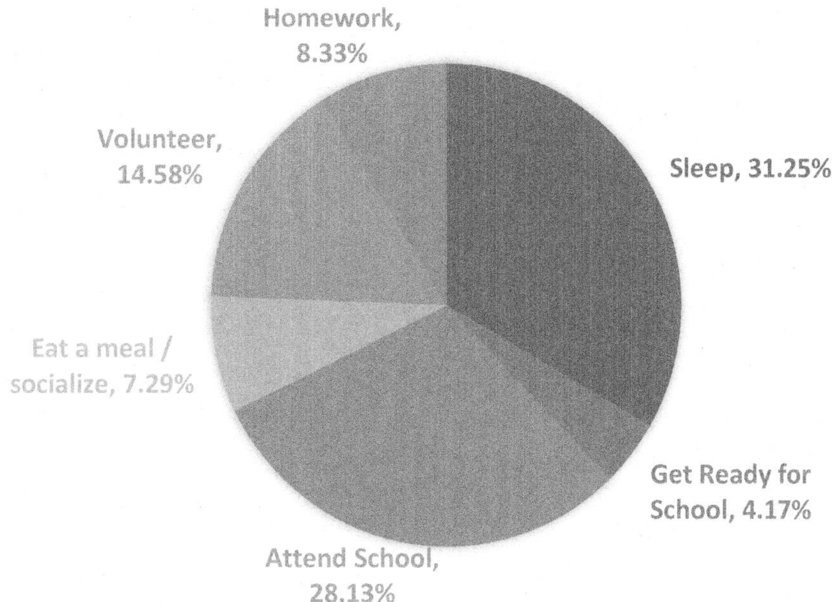

<u>Interpreting Graphs</u>

Reading and understanding graphs can be very important in all sorts of real-world fields in business, science, mathematics, medicine, law and other industries. Below, a series of practical examples will help you to review how to read and interpret results from the various graphs previously described.

Example 5: According to the graph below, is there a trend in the data? If so, what does the trend suggest? Approximately how many hours of sleep does someone who is 10 need? What ages seem to need 9 hours of sleep?

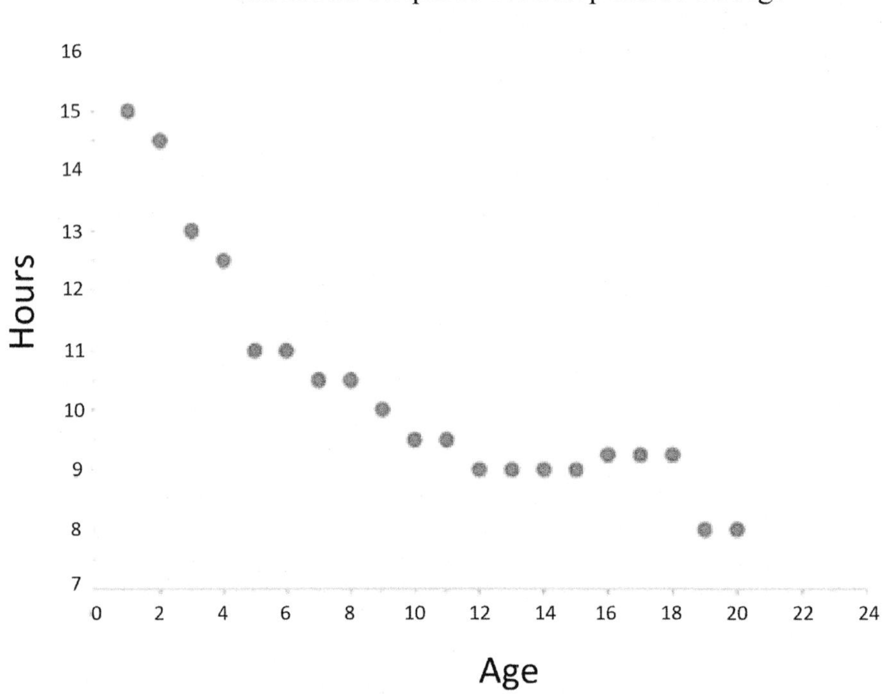

Solution:

There seems to be a linear trend (form or shape of a line) decreasing down to the right. This means that as the age increases, the hours required for sleep seem to decrease.

For someone who is 10, go to the Age axis, find 10 and locate the corresponding point. Follow it to the left and find the value on the Hours axis to be approximately 9.5. That means that a 10- year-old needs around 9.5 hours of sleep per night.

For which ages need 9 hours of sleep, locate the 9 on the Hours axis and move to the right. Notice there are four points that all line up with the 9. When you drop down to the Age axis, the range of ages is from 12 to 16. This means those in the 12 to 16-year age group need 9 hours of sleep.

Example 6: Use the line graph below to answer the questions.

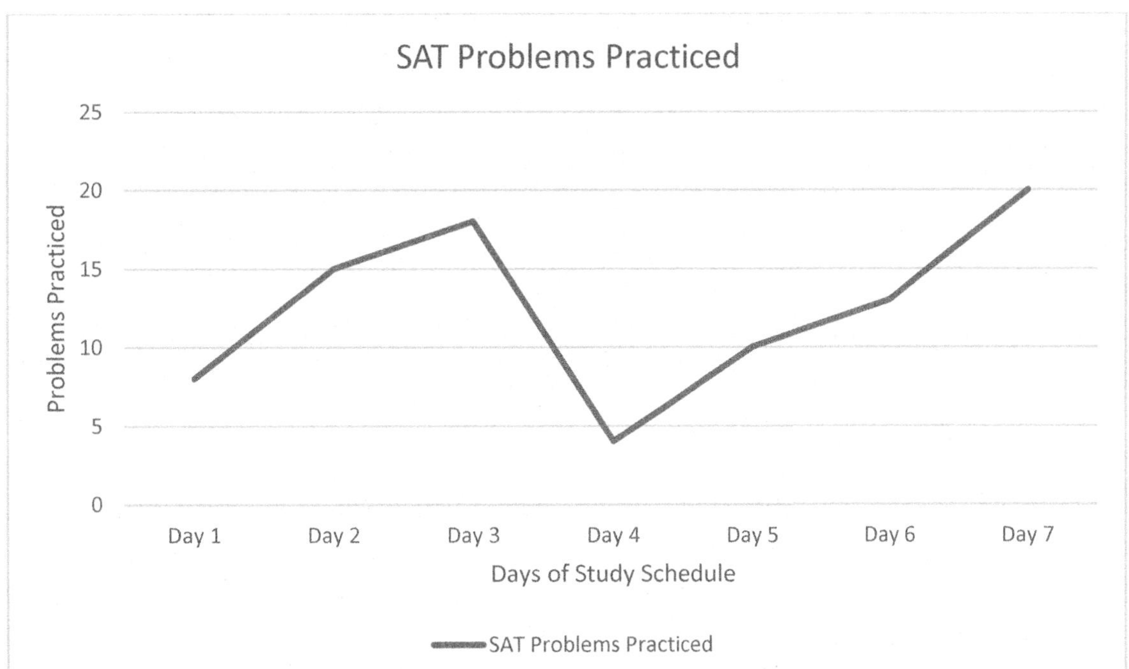

a) What is the least amount of problems the student practiced on a given day?
b) On which day did the student practice the second most amount of questions?
c) What is the range of problems the student practiced?
d) Where was the largest change in problems practiced from one day to the next? Where was the smallest change?

Solution:

a) It looks like the least number of problems is where the graph dips lowest, which is just under five problems. It can be estimated to be 4 problems were practiced on Day 4.

b) The most amount of questions were practiced on Day 7. It looks like 20 problems were practiced that day.

c) The range is the highest minus the lowest: $20 - 4 = 16$. There is a range of 16 problems practiced between the highest and lowest.

d) The largest change was from Day 3 to Day 4, when 18 problems dipped to around 4 problems, a change of -14. The smallest change was from Day 5 to Day 6. On Day 5, it seems the student practiced 10 problems but then on the next day, the student only practiced two or three more. Perhaps Day 2 to Day 3 is only a 3-problem change also, so that could be a correct answer too, depending on estimates taken from the graph.

Example 7: Use the stem-and-leaf plot below to answer questions about the data.

Stem	Leaf
1	2
2	3 3 6
3	3 4
4	6
5	0 0 3
6	2 3 4 6 6 6 7
7	1 1 2 5 8 8 8 9
8	4 5 6 9 9
9	2 3 6 9

a) If the data, put together, forms the scores for Test #3 in Professor Smith's Statistics class, how many students took the test?
b) What was the class average?
c) What was the median score?
d) Make a pie-chart from the data, divided by the following grade scale:

A: 90 – 100%; B: 80 – 89%; C: 70 – 79%; D: 60 – 69%; F: Below 60%.

Solution:

a) 34 students took the test.
b) (12 + 23 + 23 + 26 + 33 + 34 + 46 + 50 + 50 + 53 + 62 + 63 + 64 + 66 + 66 + 66 + 67 + 71 + 71 + 72 + 75 + 78 + 78 + 78 + 79 + 84 + 85 + 86 + 89 + 89 + 92 + 93 + 96 + 99) / 34 $\approx$ 65.26.
c) The very middle of all the data in ascending order is between the 67 and the 71, so take the average of the two values. The median score is: (67 + 71) / 2 = 69.
d) Make a new table of values in each grade category:

Grade Category	Frequency
A	4
B	5
C	8
D	7
F	10

Now, figure out the percentage of each grade by using the computation:

$$\frac{frequency}{total\ grades} \times 100\%$$

Grade Category	Frequency	Percentage
A	4	(4 / 34) * 100% =11.8%
B	5	(5 / 34) * 100% = 14.7%
C	8	(8 / 34) * 100% = 23.5%
D	7	(7 / 34) * 100% = 20.6%
F	10	(10/34) * 100% = 29.4%

Now, create a pie chart with the percentages and labels.

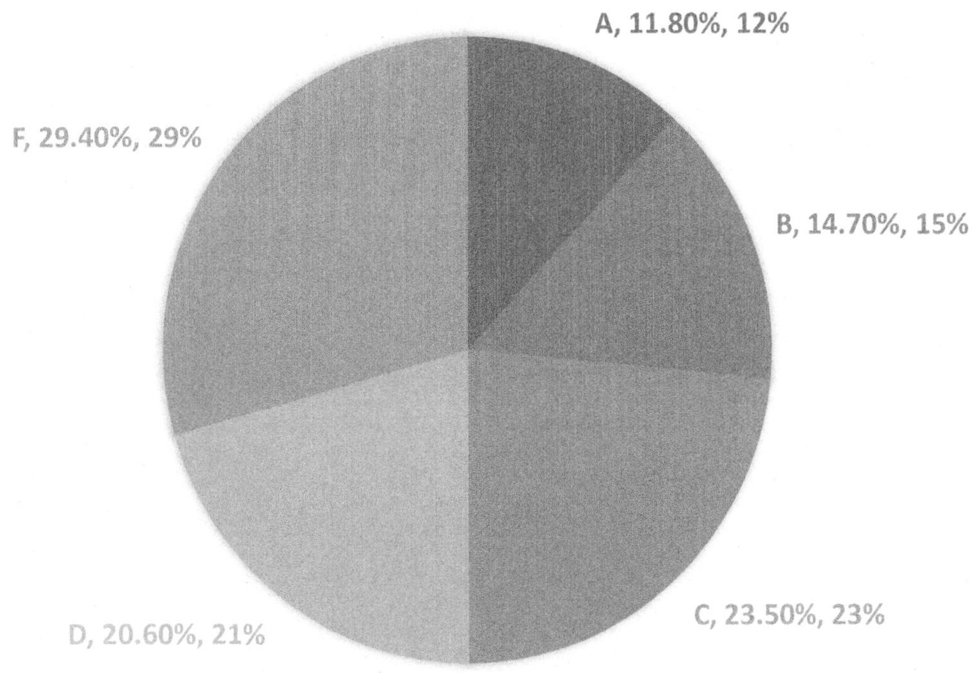

Section 16: Straight Lines and Gradients

Plotting Graphs of Straight Lines

- A **straight line** is an infinite set of points that extends indefinitely in two directions on a plane.

- A straight-line equation is called a **linear equation**. Notice the word "line" hiding in the word "linear".

- A **linear equation** will usually be given in two variables where *both variables are raised to the first power*. Some linear equations only have one variable and they'll be covered later in the lesson. When variables are raised to higher powers, you will get circles, parabolas, hyperbolas and more complicated graphs.

To **determine a specific line**, you only need **two points**.

- **Why?**
  - Draw one point on your paper. How many lines can you draw through it? Infinite? Yes. That's right. One point can have infinite lines through it, not just one line.
  - Now, draw two points on your paper. How many straight lines can you draw through both of the points? Infinite? Yes? True, but aren't they all really the same line? You can only draw the same line through the two points. So, you need two points to determine a specific, unique line.

- **Why is that good news?**
  - Since you only need two points to determine a specific line, you only have to plot two points to graph a line, so it should be very quick and easy!

Example 1: Graph each line below by plotting points in a table.

a) $y = 3x + 2$ b) $y = -\frac{1}{2}x$ c) $2x - 3y = 6$

a) It doesn't matter which x-values you choose. You will get the same line no matter what, as long as your calculations and point plotting are correct.

x	y = 3x + 2	Ordered Pair
0	y = 3(0) + 2 = **2**	(0, 2)
1	Y = 3(1) + 2 = **5**	(1, 5)

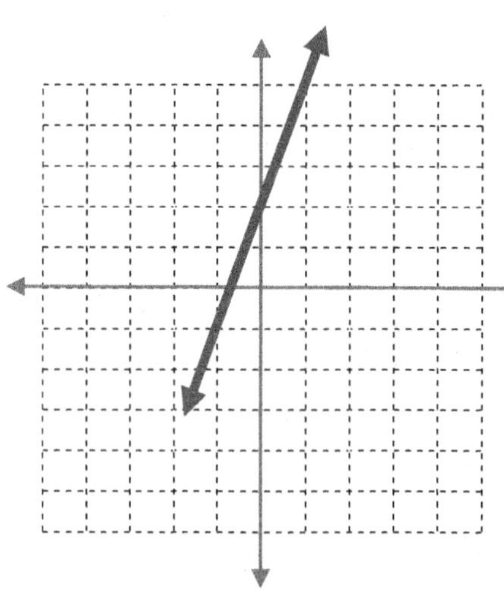

b)

x	Y = -(1/2)x	Ordered Pair
0	y = -(1/2)(0) = 0	(0, 0)
1	y = -(1/2)(1) = -1/2	(1, -1/2)

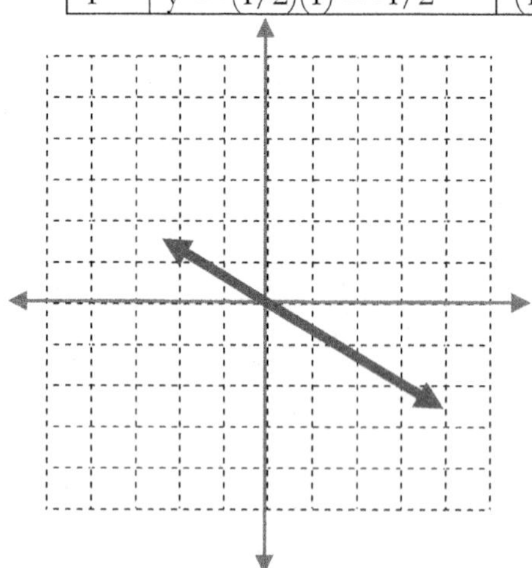

c) For this equation, you should isolate y first:

$$2x - 3y = 6 \rightarrow 2x - 2x - 3y = 6 - 2x \rightarrow -3y = 6 - 2x \rightarrow \frac{-3y}{-3} = \frac{6}{-3} - \frac{2x}{-3} \rightarrow y = -2 + \frac{2}{3}x$$

Then, plot two values in a table and graph the points, then connect in a straight line.

x	$y = -2 + \frac{2}{3}x$	Ordered Pair
0	$y = -2 + \frac{2}{3}(0) = -2$	(0, -2)
1	$y = -2 + \frac{2}{3}(1) = -4/3$	(1, -4/3)

To avoid getting a fraction, you could look at the equation and notice the "3" in the denominator of the fraction next to the "x" and then put any multiple of "3" as your "x" value to cancel it out, such as:

If x = 3: $y = -2 + \frac{2}{3}(3) = 0$, giving an ordered pair of (3, 0).

The graph would look like:

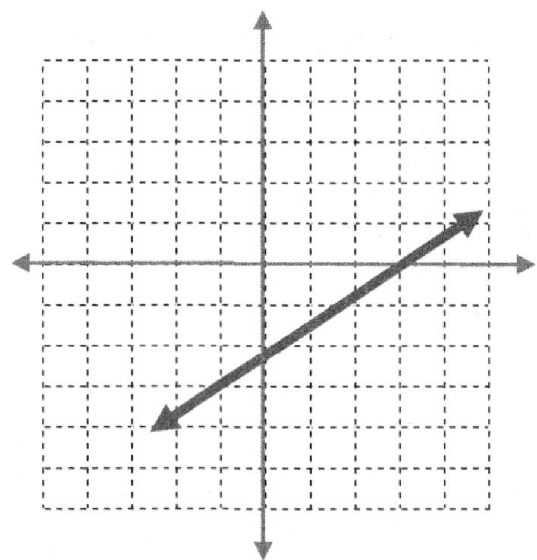

<u>Graphing a Line by Intercepts</u>
Since you only need two points to plot a specific line, you can graph by using the line's x-intercept and y-intercept. These are the ordered pairs where the line will cross the x-axis and the y-axis.

Why would I do it this way?

Unlike in the last example, with this method, ***you do not need to isolate the y variable first!*** You can just find the intercepts directly no matter how the equation is given to you.

Some people find this method easier because you're working with the number "zero".

How to graph with intercepts: To find a particular intercept, set the other variable equal to 0 and solve for the variable whose intercept you are seeking.

Example 2: Find the x-intercept and y-intercept for each equation below and graph each line.

$$a)\quad 3x + 4y = 12 \qquad\qquad b)\ y = x + 2$$

Solution:

a) For the x-intercept, set $y = 0$ and solve for x:

$$3x + 4(0) = 12 \to 3x = 12 \to x = 4 \to (4, 0) \text{ is the x-intercept.}$$

For the y-intercept, set $x = 0$ and solve for y:

$$3(0) + 4y = 12 \to 4y = 12 \to y = 3 \to (0, 3) \text{ is the y-intercept.}$$

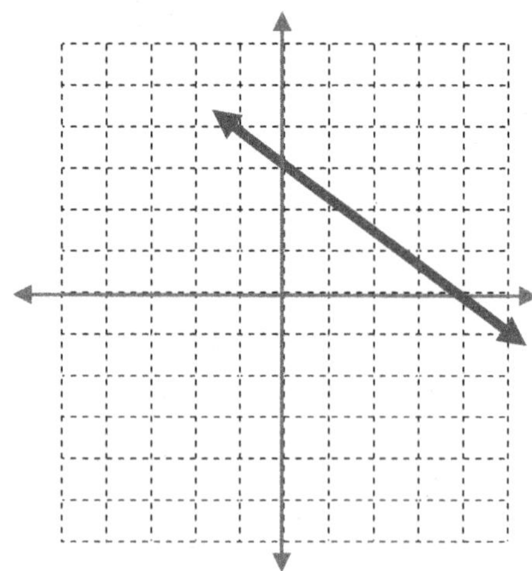

b)   For the x-intercept, set y = 0 and solve for x:

(0) = x + 2 ➜ -2 = x ➜ x = -2 ➜ (-2, 0) is the x-intercept.

y = -(0) + 2 ➜ y = 2 ➜ (0, 2) is the y-intercept.

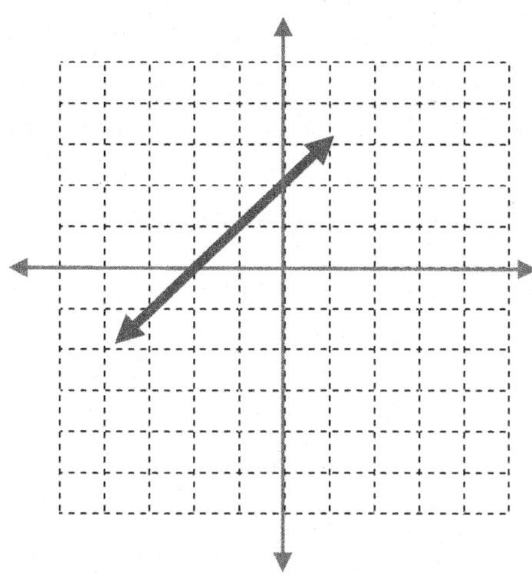

Graphing y = mx + b

A third way to graph a line is by finding the slope and the y-intercept. Once you have this information, you plot the y-intercept to find the first point and then the slope to find the second point. Remember, you still only need two points!

Step 1: Find the slope "m" and the y-intercept "b". If the equation is not already in the "y = mx + b", you'll have to solve for y first to rewrite it that way.

Step 2: Plot the point (0, b).

Step 3: Write the slope m as a fraction. If m is an integer, put it over 1 to form a fraction. If there is a negative, put it on the top or the bottom, just not both.

Now, slope m = $\dfrac{rise}{run}$, so go up or down the numerator number and then right or left the denominator number and make the second point.

Step 4: Connect your two points in a straight line.

Example 3: Use the slope and y-intercept to graph the lines y = 2x − 1 and 4x − y = 8.

Solution:

For the line y = 2x − 1, the slope is m = 2 / 1 and the y-intercept is (0, -1).

Plot the point (0, -1) and then go up 2 and right 1 and make the second point at (1, 1). Connect the points in a straight line.

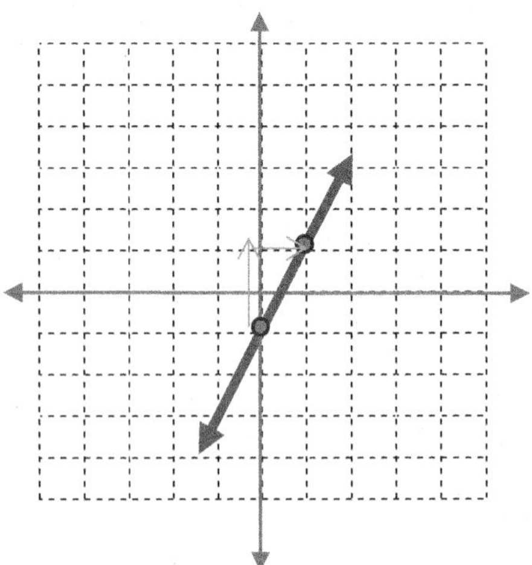

For the line 2x − y = 8, solve for y first to get it into the slope-intercept form y = mx + b:

$$4x - y = 8 \; \rightarrow \; -y = 8 - 4x \; \rightarrow \; y = -8 + 4x \; \rightarrow \; y = 4x - 8$$

Now, the slope is m = 4 / 1 and the y-intercept is (0, -8). Therefore, plot the point (0, -8). Then, go up 4 and right 1 to (1, -4).

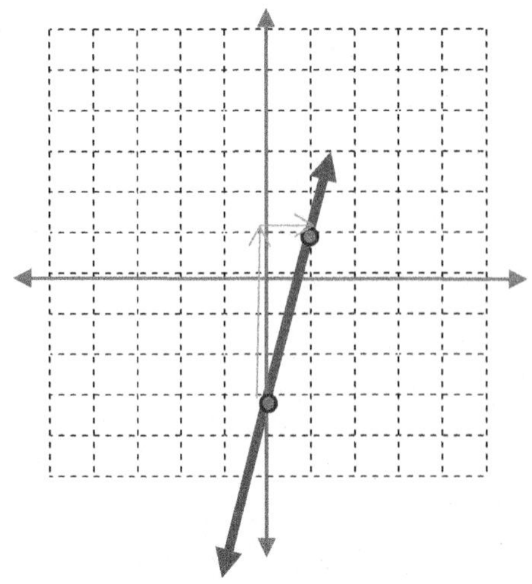

Vertical and Horizontal Lines

Vertical and horizontal line equations are the types of linear equations that only have one variable, still raised to the first power.

A **horizontal line** has the equation $\mathbf{y = k}$, where k is a real number.

A **vertical line** has the equation $\mathbf{x = b}$, where b is a real number.

How to remember the difference? When it's a horizontal line, it slices through the y-axis at $y = k$, some number. When it's a vertical line, it slices through the x-axis at $x = b$, some number.

Example 4: Graph the lines x = -2 and y = 5.

Solution:

To graph the line x = -2, notice it slices through the x-axis at -2. That means it is vertical.

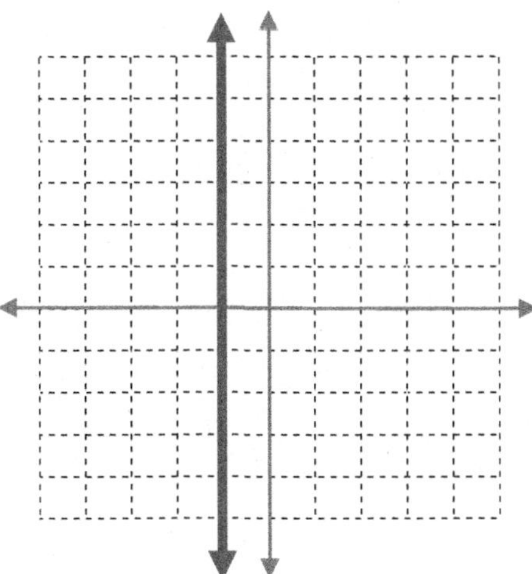

To graph the line y = 5, notice it slices through the y-axis at 5. That means it is horizontal.

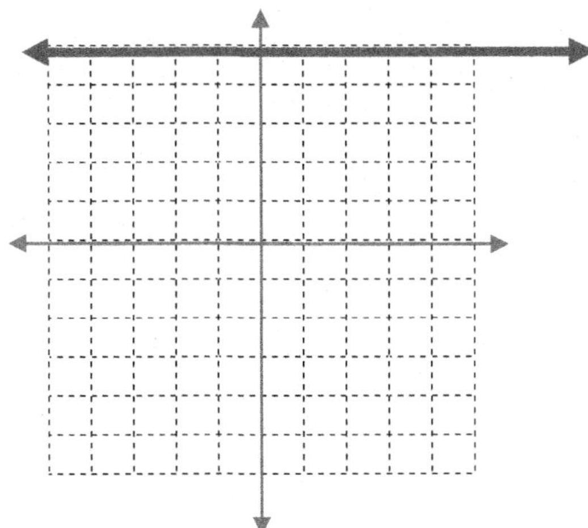

<u>Slope of a Line</u>

The **slope or gradient** of a line is the incline of a line. It can be positive, negative, zero or undefined. This gives the average rate of change between the two variables.

The **slope between any two points** (x_1, y_1) and (x_2, y_2): $m = \dfrac{rise}{run} = \dfrac{y_2 - y_1}{x_2 - x_1}$.

Note: It does not matter which of your points is designated (x_1, y_1) with this formula because the slope between two points is the same no matter which you start with. Try to make the slope calculation with each point as your initial point and you should get the same answer!

How to remember? A good way to remember the y's go in the numerator in the formula is to realize "y's" rhymes with "rise".

Example 5: Find the slope of the line between each set of points. Graph the lines.

    a)   (2, -3) and (-4, 5)   b) (-1, 3) and (-1, -2)   c) (2, 4) and (5, 4)

Solution:

    a) Let $(x_1, y_1) = (2, -3)$ and $(x_2, y_2) = (-4, 5)$. Then, $m = \dfrac{5 - (-3)}{(-4) - 2} = \dfrac{8}{-6} = -\dfrac{4}{3}$

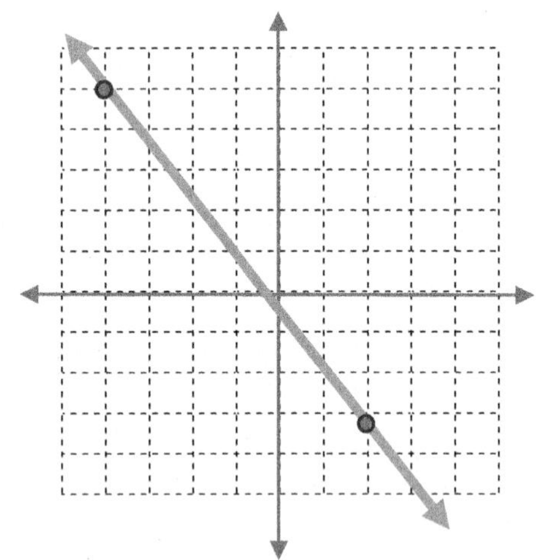

b) Let $(x_1, y_1) = (-1, 3)$ and $(x_2, y_2) = (-1, -2)$. Then, $m = \frac{-2-3}{(-1)-(-1)} = \frac{-5}{0} =$ *undefined*

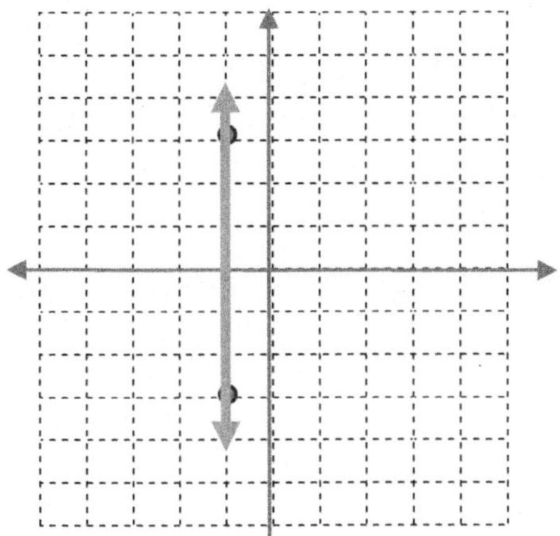

Notice when the x-values in the coordinates are the same and the slope is undefined in the calculation, this is for a vertical line. All vertical lines have undefined slopes.

c) Let $(x_1, y_1) = (2, 4)$ and $(x_2, y_2) = (5, 4)$. Then, $m = \frac{4-4}{5-4} = \frac{0}{1} = 0$.

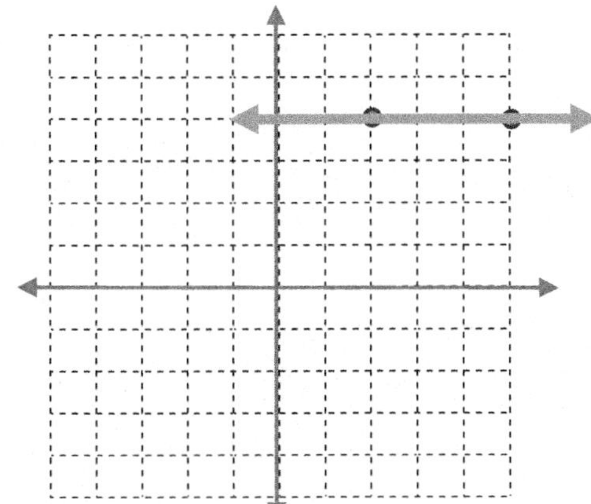

Notice when the y-coordinates are the same, the line is horizontal and has a zero slope.

Helpful Tip: Which is undefined, $\frac{1}{0}$ or $\frac{0}{1}$?

- You can think of the "zero" like an egg.
- If the "egg" is on top, it lives: $\frac{0}{1} = 0$.
- If the "egg" is on the bottom, it gets crushed: $\frac{1}{0} = undefined$

<u>Equation of a Line</u>

You can find the slope-intercept equation (y = mx + b) of a line from any two points on the line by doing the following:

Step 1: Find the slope using the slope formula as you did above.

Step 2: Choose either point – it doesn't matter – and plug in the x and y values into the y = mx+b equation and solve for b,

Step 3: Write the equation with x and y as variables but plug in the values for 3m and b.

Example 6: Find the equation of the line through the points (1, -3) and (-2 ,4).

Solution:

Step 1: The slope of the line is $m = \dfrac{4-(-3)}{-2-1} = \dfrac{7}{-3} = -\dfrac{7}{3}$.

Plug that value into the equation. $y = -\dfrac{7}{3}x + b$.

Step 2: Plug in the point (1, -3) ➜ (-3) = (-7/3)(1) + b ➜ -3 + (7/3) = b ➜ b = -2/3

Step 3: $y = -\dfrac{7}{3}x - \dfrac{2}{3}$ is the equation of the line through the points.

Section 17: Functions

A function is a relation between two variables where for every x-value, there is exactly one corresponding y-value.

Example 1: Determine if each equation represents a function.

    a) $2y = 3x + 4$ b) $2y = 3x^2 + 4$ c) $2y^2 = 3x + 4$

Solution:

a) For the equation $2y = 3x + 4$, no matter which x-value you plug in, when you solve for y, you will only get one y-value. Try it with different x-values to see!

    Try x = 2: $2y = 3(2) + 4$ ➜ 2y = 10 ➜ y = 5 ➜ only one y-value
    Try x = -7: $2y = 3(-7) + 4$ ➜ 2y = -17 ➜ y = -17/2 ➜ only one y-value
    Try x = 31: $2y = 3(31) + 4$ ➜ 2y = 97 ➜ y = 97/2 ➜ only one y-value

You can input x-values for the rest of your life and you'll always only get one corresponding y-value. Since no matter which x-value you put in, you only get one y-value each time, y is a function of x.

b) For the equation $2y = 3x^2 + 4$, same as in the previous example, no matter which x-value you plug in, you'll get a different y-value. Try any x-values to see! You can organize your values in a table. Since no matter which x-value you put in, you only get one y-value, y is a function of x.

x (put any value you want)	$y = \dfrac{3x^2 + 4}{2}$
0	2
1	7/2
-1	7/2 (two different x-values with same y)
17	435.5
-100	15,002

c) For the equation $2y^2 = 3x + 4$, to solve for the y:

$$2y^2 = 3x + 4 \;➜\; y^2 = \frac{3x+4}{2} \;➜\; y = \pm\sqrt{\frac{3x+4}{2}}$$

(Recall the **Square Root Property**, which says if $u^2 = k$, where k is a real number and u is an algebraic expression of x, then $u = \pm\sqrt{k}$). Now, for any x you plug in, you will get two y-values.

For example, if x = 0: $y = \pm\sqrt{\frac{3(0)+4}{2}} = \pm\sqrt{2}$. Thus, For x = 0, there are two y-values assigned.

Therefore, $2y^2 = 3x + 4$ is not a function.

Important tip: In any equation, if the "y" variable (or whatever the vertical variable is called) is squared or to any even power, the equation is not a function of your horizontal variable!

Evaluating Functions with Function Notation

Function Notation: Functions can be written with variables x and y, and they often are, but a more helpful way to write them is with something called **function notation**.

    y = 3x + 1   >>>>>> this statement says >>>>>>> y is a function of x

Recall in math, "is" means "=". Instead of writing "a function of x", we can shorten that to write "f(x)", pronounced "f of x" to mean **a function called f with an input of variable x.**

    y = 3x + 1   >>>>>> you can write >>>>>>> y = f(x)

So, y = 3x + 1 can be rewritten as f(x) = 3x + 1.

Why is function notation needed? There are two advantages. First, it tells you what the input variable is. "f(x)" tells you the input is called "x" and "p(t)" tells you the input is called "t", whereas if it's just called "y", you have no idea what the input is! Second, you can differentiate the purpose for functions by giving then different letters. For example, for a cost function and a revenue function, instead of calling them both "y =", one could be called "R(x)" and the other could be called "C(x)". Function notation is more descriptive and helpful.

Example 2: Let $f(x) = 3 - 2x - 4x^2$, $g(x) = \frac{3x}{5x+2}$, $h(x) = 2x - \sqrt{2 - x}$. Evaluate each function for the given input values. Simplify completely. What does your answer mean for each?

    a) f(-3)   b) $g\left(\frac{4}{5}\right)$ c) $h(-7)$ d) $h(3)$

Solution:
    a) f(-3) means go to the "f" function and give it an input of "-3". Everywhere you see the "x", put in a "-3", making sure to use parentheses.

$$f(-3) = 3 - 2(-3) - 4(-3)^2$$
$$= 3 - 2(-3) - 4(9)$$
$$= 3 + 6 - 36 = 9 - 36 = -27$$

    This means that the point (-3, -27) is a point on the graph of f(x).

b) $g\left(\frac{4}{5}\right) = \dfrac{3\left(\frac{4}{5}\right)}{5\left(\frac{4}{5}\right)+2} = \dfrac{\frac{12}{5}}{\frac{20}{5}+\frac{10}{5}} = \dfrac{\frac{12}{5}}{\frac{30}{5}} = \dfrac{\frac{12}{5}}{6} = \dfrac{12}{5} \times \dfrac{1}{6} = \dfrac{2}{5}$

This means that the point $\left(\frac{4}{5},\frac{2}{5}\right)$ is on the function g(x).

c) $h(-7) = 2(-7) - \sqrt{2-(-7)} = -14 - \sqrt{9} = -14 - 3 = -17.$

This means that the point (-7, -17) is on h(x).

d) $h(3) = 2(3) - \sqrt{2-(3)} = 6 - \sqrt{-1} = 6 - i.$ Since the output is not a real number, there is no point on the graph of h(x) that has an x value of 3.

Combining Functions

Operations on Functions: Just like with numbers, with functions you can **add, subtract, multiply** and **divide** them. However, there is a fifth operation you can do on functions, something called **function composition**.

Definitions:
1) **Addition:** $(f + g)(x) = f(x) + g(x)$
2) **Subtraction:** $(f - g)(x) = f(x) - g(x)$
3) **Multiplication:** $(fg)(x) = f(x)g(x)$
4) **Division:** $(f/g)(x) = f(x)/g(x), g(x) \neq 0$
5) **Function Composition:** $(f \circ g)(x) = f(g(x))$

Example 3: Let $f(x) = \dfrac{2-3\sqrt{x}}{2x}$, $g(x) = 1 - 5x - 7x^2$, $k(x) = 3x + 4$. Say what the meaning is of each.

    a) Find $(g - k)(-1)$.
    b) Find $(k + g)(2)$.
    c) Find $(fk)(4)$.
    d) Find $\left(\frac{g}{f}\right)(4)$.
    e) Find $(g \circ f)(1)$.
    f) Find $(f \circ f)(25)$.

Solution:

a) $(g - k)(-1) = g(-1) - k(-1) = (1 - 5(-1) - 7(-1)^2) - (3(-1) + 4)$

$$= \left(1 - 5(-1) - 7(1)\right) - (-3 + 4)$$
$$= (1 + 5 - 7) - (1) = 6 - 7 - 1 = -1 - 1 = -2.$$

This means that (-1, -2) is a point on the graph of the function $(g - k)(x)$.

b) $(k + g)(2) = k(2) + g(2) = (3(2) + 4) + (1 - 5(2) - 7(2)^2)$

$$= (10) + \left(1 - 5(2) - 7(4)\right)$$
$$= (10) + (1 - 10 - 28)$$
$$= (10) + (9 - 28) = 10 - 19 = -9$$

This means that (2, -9) is a point on the graph of the function $(k + g)(x)$.

c) $(fk)(4) = f(4)k(4) = \frac{2-3\sqrt{4}}{2(4)}(3(4) + 4) = \frac{2-3(2)}{8}(16) = -\frac{1}{2}(16) = -8$

This means that (4, -8) is a point on the graph of the function $(fk)(x)$.

d) $\left(\frac{g}{f}\right)(4) = \frac{g(4)}{f(4)} = \frac{(1-5(4)-7(4)^2)}{\frac{2-3\sqrt{4}}{2(4)}} = \frac{(1-5(4)-7(16))}{\frac{2-3(2)}{8}} = \frac{(1-20-112))}{\frac{-4}{8}} = \frac{-131}{\frac{-1}{2}} = -131(-2) = 262.$

This means that (4, 262) is a point on the graph of the function $(g/f)(x)$.

e) $(g \circ f)(1) = g(f(1)) = g\left(\frac{2-3\sqrt{1}}{2(1)}\right) = g\left(\frac{2-3}{2}\right) = g\left(\frac{-1}{2}\right) = 1 - 5\left(-\frac{1}{2}\right) - 7\left(-\frac{1}{2}\right)^2 =$

$1 - 5\left(-\frac{1}{2}\right) - 7\left(\frac{1}{4}\right) = 1 + \frac{5}{2} - \frac{7}{4} = \frac{4}{4} + \frac{10}{4} - \frac{7}{4} = \frac{7}{4}.$

This means that (1, 7/4) is a point on the graph of the function $(g \circ f)(x)$.

f) $(f \circ f)(25) = f(f(25)) = f\left(\frac{2-3\sqrt{25}}{2(25)}\right) = f\left(\frac{2-3(5)}{50}\right) = f\left(\frac{-13)}{50}\right) = \frac{2-3\sqrt{\frac{-13)}{50}}}{2\left(\frac{-13)}{50}\right)} = \text{und.}$

This means that there is no corresponding real y-value for an x-value of 25 on the graph of $(f \circ f)(x)$.

  Let $f(x) = 4x^2 - 2x$, $k(x) = \frac{2x+5}{9-5x}$, $p(x) = 6\sqrt{8x+1}$.

Find each of the following, simplifying completely:

a) $(f - k)(x)$

b) $\left(\frac{p}{k}\right)(x)$

c) $(k \circ k)(x)$.

Describe the meaning of each.

Solution:

a) To find $(f - k)(x)$, always use the definition: $(f - k)(x) = f(x) - k(x)$

Then, plug in each function:

$$= (4x^2 - 2x) - \left(\frac{2x+5}{9-5x}\right)$$

To simplify, we must get a LCD:

$$= \frac{4x^2 - 2x}{1}\left(\frac{9-5x}{9-5x}\right) - \frac{2x+5}{9-5x} = \frac{36x^2 - 20x^3 - 18x + 10x^2}{9-5x} + \frac{-2x-5}{9-5x}$$

$$= \frac{-20x^3 + 46x^2 - 20x - 5}{9-5x}$$

Then, we check if there are any terms besides 1 we can factor from the numerator or denominator. It seems the numerator and denominator are fully factored, so the fraction is fully reduced.

This means that $\left(x, \frac{-20x^3 + 46x^2 - 20x - 5}{9-5x}\right)$ are infinite points on the graph of $(f - k)(x)$.

b) To find $\left(\frac{p}{k}\right)(x)$, always use the definition:

$$\left(\frac{p}{k}\right)(x) = \frac{p(x)}{k(x)}$$

Then, plug in each function:

$$= \frac{6\sqrt{8x+1}}{\frac{2x+5}{9-5x}}$$

To simplify, multiply by the reciprocal:

$$= \frac{6\sqrt{8x+1}}{1} \cdot \frac{9-5x}{2x+5}$$

Nothing will cancel with the "6" and the "2x + 5", but no reason to multiply the "6" and the "9 – 5x", so just leave them separate.

$$= \frac{6(9-5x)\sqrt{8x+1}}{2x+5}$$

This means that $\left(x, \frac{6(9-5x)\sqrt{8x+1}}{2x+5}\right)$ are infinite points on the graph of (p/k)(x).

c) To find $(k \circ k)(x)$, you want to plug the "k" function into itself. Always start with the function composition definition.

$$(k \circ k)(x) = k\big(k(x)\big) = k\left(\frac{2x+5}{9-5x}\right)$$

Now, where you see the variable "x", insert the function k(x):

$$= \frac{2\left(\frac{2x+5}{9-5x}\right)+5}{9-5\left(\frac{2x+5}{9-5x}\right)}$$

In the numerator, get an LCD. Do the same in the denominator.

$$= \frac{\frac{2}{1}\left(\frac{2x+5}{9-5x}\right)+\frac{5}{1}\left(\frac{9-5x}{9-5x}\right)}{\frac{9}{1}\left(\frac{9-5x}{9-5x}\right)-\frac{5}{1}\left(\frac{2x+5}{9-5x}\right)} = \frac{\left(\frac{4x+10}{9-5x}\right)+\left(\frac{45-25x}{9-5x}\right)}{\left(\frac{81-45x}{9-5x}\right)-\left(\frac{10x+25}{9-5x}\right)} = \frac{\frac{4x+10+45-25x}{9-5x}}{\frac{81-45x-10x-25}{9-5x}} = \frac{\frac{-21x+55}{9-5x}}{\frac{-55x+56}{9-5x}}$$

Multiply by the reciprocal and simplify if possible.

$$= \frac{-21x+55}{9-5x} \cdot \frac{9-5x}{-55x+56} = \frac{-21x+55}{-55x+56}$$

This means that there are infinite points of the form $\left(x, \frac{-21x+55}{-55x+56}\right)$ on the graph of the function $(k \circ k)(x)$.

<u>Inverse Functions</u>

Two functions are **inverses** if they trade each other's x and y values. How to determine if f and g are inverses:

      1) Prove $(f \circ g)(x) = x$.
      2) Prove $(g \circ f)(x) = x$.

If you show one composition is not x, you do not need to show the other way because you already know the two functions are not inverses.

Note: If f and g are inverses, they are unique. This means that f cannot have another inverse also that trades its x and y values. If g is its inverse, no other function can be. You can think of f and g like "soulmates": they will only be together forever and cannot be with others.

Example 5: Determine if the functions are unique inverses.

a) $f(x) = 4x^3 - 7$ and $g(x) = \sqrt[3]{\dfrac{x+7}{4}}$

b) $f(x) = \dfrac{2x+6}{x-3}$ and $g(x) = \dfrac{3x+6}{x-2}$

Solution:

a) $(f \circ g)(x) = f(g(x)) = f\left(\sqrt[3]{\dfrac{x+7}{4}}\right) = 4\left(\sqrt[3]{\dfrac{x+7}{4}}\right)^3 - 7 = 4\left(\dfrac{x+7}{4}\right) - 7 = x + 7 - 7 = x$

$$(g \circ f)(x) = g(f(x)) = g(4x^3 - 7) = \sqrt[3]{\dfrac{(4x^3 - 7) + 7}{4}} = \sqrt[3]{\dfrac{4x^3}{4}} = \sqrt[3]{x^3} = x$$

Therefore, f and g are unique inverses.

b) $(f \circ g)(x) = f(g(x)) = f\left(\dfrac{3x+6}{x-2}\right) = \dfrac{2\left(\frac{3x+6}{x-2}\right)+6}{\left(\frac{3x+6}{x-2}\right)-3} = \dfrac{\left(\frac{6x+12}{x-2}\right)+\frac{6x-12}{x-2}}{\left(\frac{3x+6}{x-2}\right)-\frac{3(x-2)}{x-2}}$

$$= \dfrac{\dfrac{12x}{x-2}}{\dfrac{12}{x-2}} = \dfrac{12x}{x-2} \cdot \dfrac{x-2}{12} = x$$

$(g \circ f)(x) = g(f(x)) = g\left(\dfrac{2x+6}{x-3}\right) = \dfrac{3\left(\frac{2x+6}{x-3}\right)+6}{\left(\frac{2x+6}{x-3}\right)-2} = \dfrac{\left(\frac{6x+18}{x-3}\right)+\frac{6x-18}{x-3}}{\left(\frac{2x+6}{x-3}\right)-\frac{2(x-3)}{x-3}}$

$$= \dfrac{\dfrac{12x}{x-3}}{\dfrac{12}{x-3}} = \dfrac{12x}{x-3} \cdot \dfrac{x-3}{12} = x$$

Finding the Inverse of a Function

To find the inverse of a function, follow the procedure below:

> **Step 1**: Write "f(x)" or any other function notation as "y".
> **Step 2**: Switch "x" and "y" variables.
> **Step 3**: Solve for y.
> **Step 4**: Replace "y" with "$f^{-1}(x)$", or whatever your function name is, the little "-1" superscript meaning "inverse".

Example 6: Find the inverse for the function $f(x) = 3x^5 - 2$. Verify the two functions are inverses.

Solution:

Step 1: $y = 3x^5 - 2$

Step 2: $x = 3y^5 - 2$

Step 3: $x + 2 = 3y^5 - 2 + 2 \rightarrow \dfrac{x+2}{3} = \dfrac{3y^5}{3} \rightarrow \sqrt[5]{\dfrac{x+2}{3}} = \sqrt[5]{y^5} \rightarrow \sqrt[5]{\dfrac{x+2}{3}} = y$

Step 4: $f^{-1}(x) = \sqrt[5]{\dfrac{x+2}{3}}$

To verify if they are inverses, we must show that $(f \circ f^{-1})(x) = x$ and $(f^{-1} \circ f)(x) = x$.

$$(f \circ f^{-1})(x) = f(f^{-1}(x)) = f\left(\sqrt[5]{\dfrac{x+2}{3}}\right) = 3\left(\sqrt[5]{\dfrac{x+2}{3}}\right)^5 - 2 = 3\left(\dfrac{x+2}{3}\right) - 2 = x + 2 - 2 = x$$

and

$$(f^{-1} \circ f)(x) = (f^{-1}f(x)) = (f^{-1}(3x^5 - 2)) = \sqrt[5]{\dfrac{(3x^5 - 2) + 2}{3}} = \sqrt[5]{\dfrac{3x^5}{3}} = \sqrt[5]{x^5} = x$$

Therefore, we found the right inverse and f and g are each other's only inverse.

Section 18: Exponential Graphs

<u>Quadratic / Squaring Graph $y = x^2$</u>

To graph this basic function, you can plot points in a table.

X	$y = x^2$
0	$y = (0)^2 = 0$
1	$y = (1)^2 = 1$
2	$y = (2)^2 = 4$
-1	$y = (-1)^2 = 1$
-2	$y = (-2)^2 = 4$

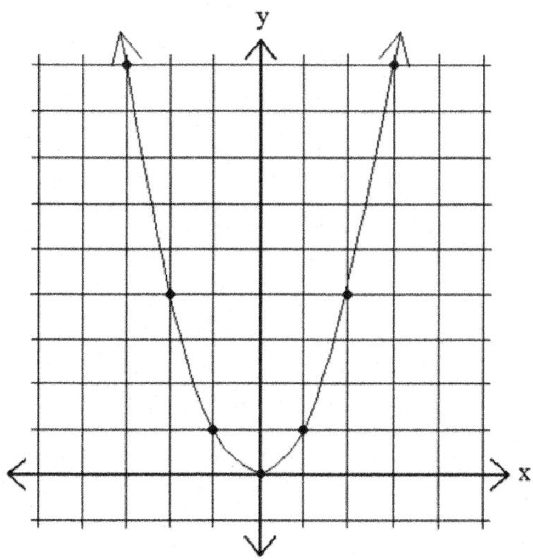

When you do, you can see the shape is an upward-facing parabola. Some people describe this as a "u-shaped" curve.

<u>Transforming the Squaring Graph</u>
- To move the graph $f(x) = x^2$ **up c units,** $g(x) = f(x) + c = x^2 + c$
- To move the graph $f(x) = x^2$ **down c units,** $g(x) = f(x) - c = x^2 - c$
- To move the graph $f(x) = x^2$ **right c units,** $g(x) = f(x - c) = (x - c)^2$
- To move the graph $f(x) = x^2$ **left c units,** $g(x) = f(x + c) = (x + c)^2$

Note: For the right and left shifting, the sign is opposite what you would expect! That is not a mistake. It is actually the opposite!

- To **reflect the graph** $f(x) = x^2$ **over the x-axis,** $g(x) = -f(x) = -x^2$.
- To **reflect the graph** $f(x) = x^2$ **over the y-axis,** $g(x) = f(-x) = (-x)^2$.

Order of Graphing: Order doesn't matter too much, but it's best to do any reflections first before any shifting right, left, up or down.

Example 1: Name the basic function and all transformations you see for each composite function.

a) $g(x) = -(x - 3)^2 + 1$ b) $g(x) = (-x + 5)^2 - 4$

Solution:

a) To find the basic function, locate your variable. It is raised to the second power. The rest of the numbers and signs don't matter. The basic function is $y = x^2$.

The negative sign in front of the quantity squared means the function is reflected over the x-axis.

The "-3" means to move right three. The "+1" means to move up 1.

b) A very important note to be made here because notice that the negative sign is on the variable but not on the 5? The negative sign needs to be applied to all terms inside the function. This is something implied in the rule but not obvious at all!

So, rewrite the function like this: $g(x) = (-(x - 5))^2 - 4$
Factoring out the negative so it is applied
to both the "x" and the "5" now.

The basic function is still the $y = x^2$. The negative sign inside the parentheses means the function is reflecting on the y-axis. Since a parabola has y-axis symmetry, if it does so, it'll land right on itself!

The "-5" now means go "right 5". Many who forgot the important note at the top of this may have said "left 5" mistakenly, forgetting to factor out the negative. A very easy mistake to make if you're not careful!

The "-4" means go "down 4".

: Graph each of the functions in Example 1 by first graphing and labelling the basic function and then graphing and labelling each additional function.

$$f(x) = x^2$$

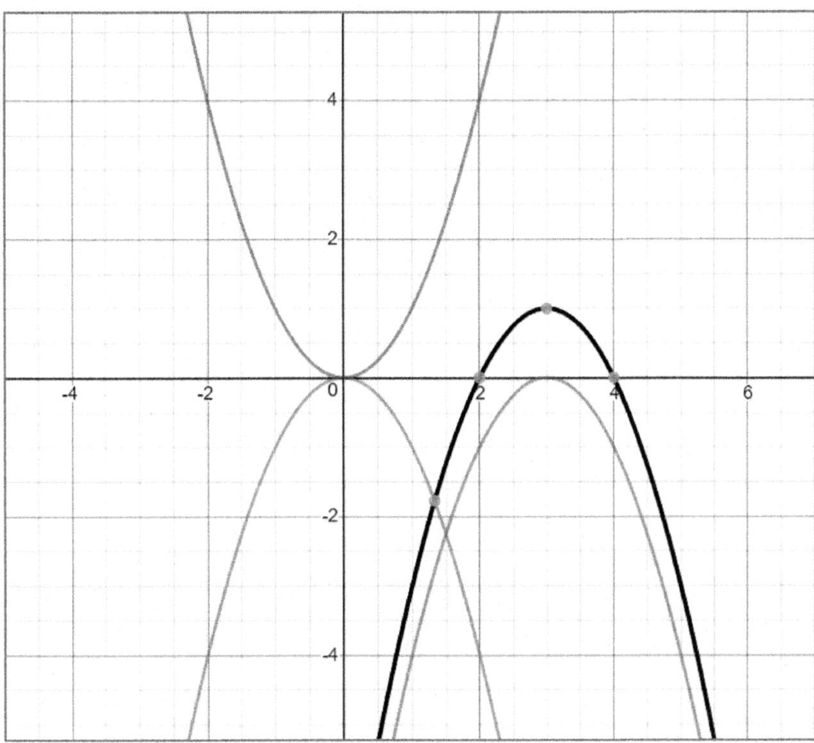

$$f(x) = -x^2 \qquad\qquad f(x) = -(x-3)^2 \qquad\qquad f(x) = (x-3)^2 + 1$$

b) $\qquad$ $f(x) = x^2 = (-x)^2$ $\qquad$ $f(x) = (-(x-5))^2$ $\qquad$ $f(x) = (-(x-5))^2 - 4$

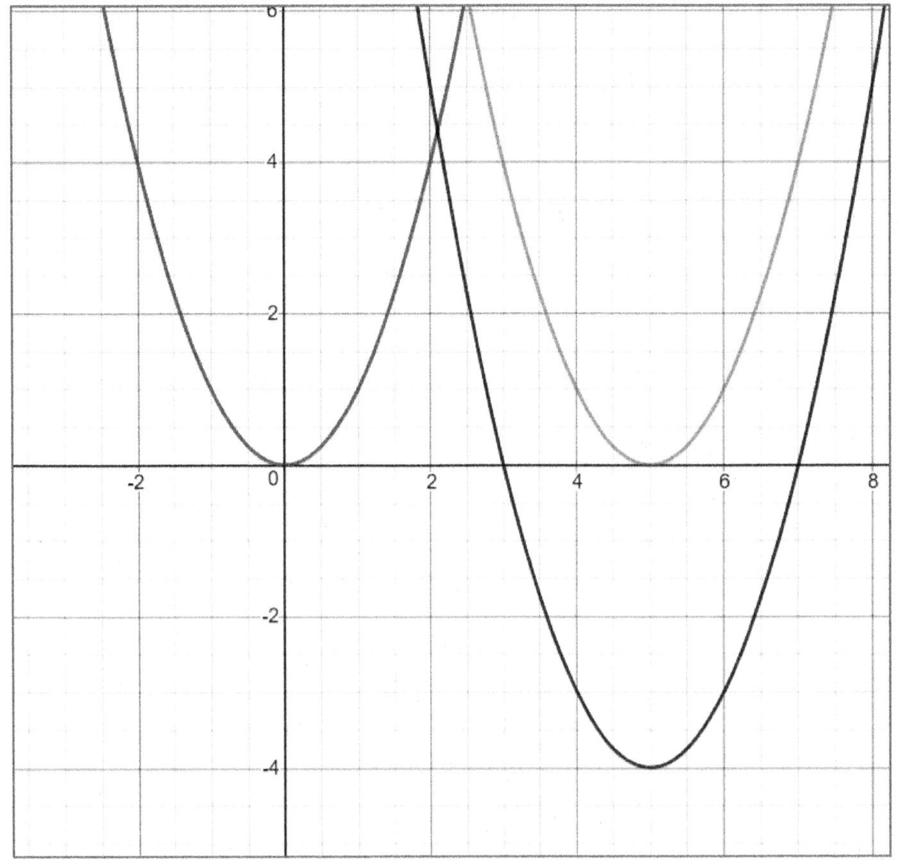

The Cubic Graph $y = x^3$

To graph this basic function, you can plot points in a table.

x	$y = x^3$
0	$y = (0)^3 = 0$
1	$y = (1)^3 = 1$
2	$y = (2)^3 = 8$
-1	$y = (-1)^3 = -1$
-2	$y = (-2)^3 = -8$

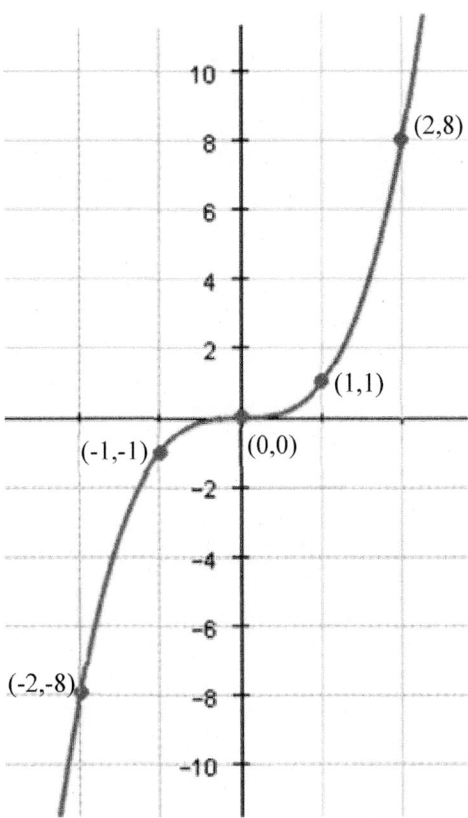

The Cubic Graph $y = x^3$

<u>Transformations</u>

Quadratic graphs, X3 graphs, Circle graphs, 1/x graph s, exponential graphs (I anticipate this section will require 3-4 pages for review, and I need TWO practice questions per graph type, so 10 questions for this last topic).

Transforming the Cubing Graph:
- To move the graph $f(x) = x^3$ **up c units**, $g(x) = f(x) + c = x^3 + c$
- To move the graph $f(x) = x^3$ **down c units**, $g(x) = f(x) - c = x^3 - c$
- To move the graph $f(x) = x^3$ **right c units**, $g(x) = f(x - c) = (x - c)^3$
- To move the graph $f(x) = x^3$ **left c units**, $g(x) = f(x + c) = (x + c)^3$

Note: For the right and left shifting, the sign is opposite what you would expect! That is not a mistake. It is actually the opposite!
- To **reflect the graph** $f(x) = x^3$ **over the x-axis, $g(x) = -f(x)$.**
- To **reflect the graph** $f(x) = x^3$ **over the y-axis, $g(x) = f(-x)$.**

Order of Graphing: Order doesn't matter too much, but it's best to do any reflections first before any shifting right, left, up or down.

Example 4: Graph $f(x) = -(-x - 5)^3 - 2$. First, identify and graph and label your basic function. Then, identify each transformation to the basic function and graph it and label it. Do reflections before shifting.

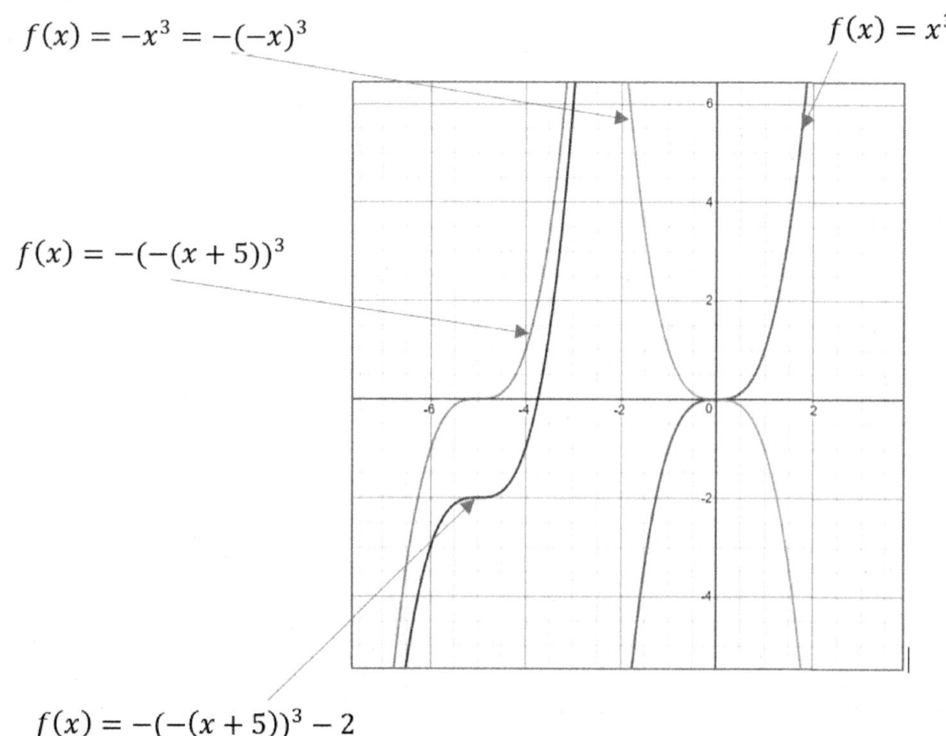

<u>Circles</u>

Any equation of the form $(x - h)^2 + (y - k)^2 = r^2$ is a **circle** with a center of (h, k) and a radius $r \geq 0$. This equation is considered the **standard form equation of a circle.**

- **Note:** The coordinates of the center are the opposite signs of what is in the equation.
- **Note:** If the r-value is negative, it is not a circle. If the r-value is 0, it's not a circle but simply a point, namely the center of the circle (h, k).

- **To recognize a circle equation:** Look for both **x and y to be squared, to be added together** and **have the same coefficients.** Otherwise, it may be another type of graph besides a circle.

Example 5: Find the center and radius of each circle. Graph each circle.

a) $(x - 2)^2 + (y + 1)^2 = 25$ 　　　　　b) $(x + 4)^2 + y^2 = 9$

Solution:

a) The center is always the opposite signs than what is given in the equation. So, the center is (h,k) = (2, -1). The radius is: $r^2 = 25 \rightarrow r = \pm 5$. But, the radius cannot be negative, so r = 5.

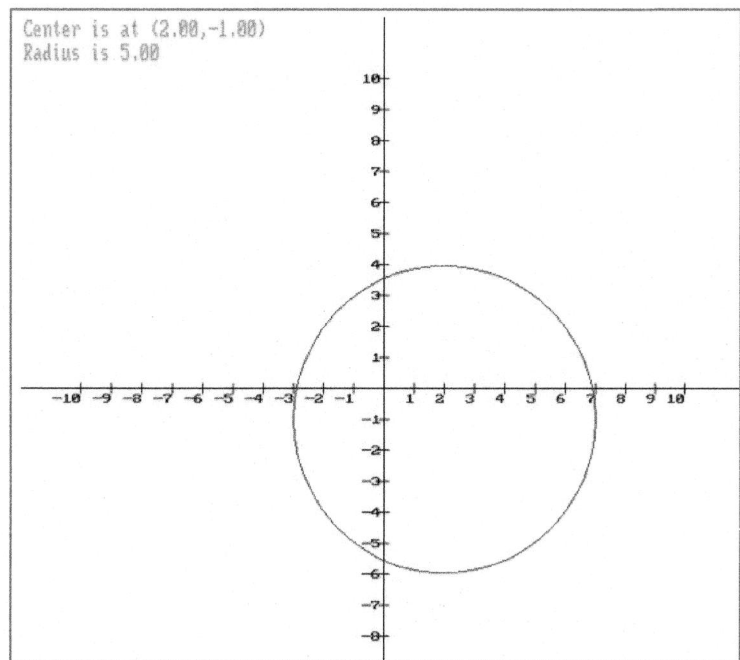

b) The center is always the opposite signs than what is given in the equation. Notice with the y^2 that it seems the "- k" is missing, but it's not! If you don't see it, you can assume the value is 0. So, $y^2 = (y - 0)^2$. Therefore, the center of this circle is (-4, 0).

The radius is: $r^2 = 9$➔$r = \pm 3$ ➔ r = 3 since the radius is non-negative.

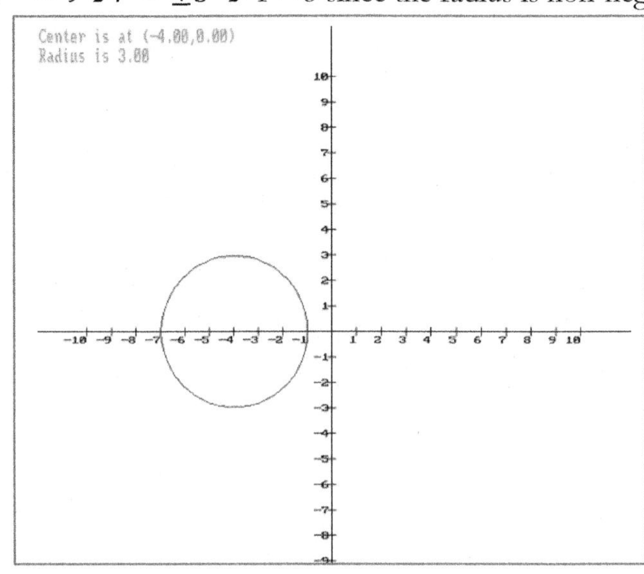

Example 5: Find the standard equations of the circles with the following information below.

    a) Center: (0, 3), Radius: $2\sqrt{7}$ b) Center: $(-4, 1)$, Radius: $\frac{3}{2}$

Solution:

    a) $(x - h)^2 + (y - k)^2 = r^2$ ➔

Plug in the (h, k) = (0, 3) and r = $2\sqrt{7}$: $(x - (0))^2 + (y - (3))^2 = (2\sqrt{7})^2$
➔ $x^2 + (y - 3)^2 = (4)(7)$ ➔ $x^2 + (y - 3)^2 = 28$

    b) $(x - h)^2 + (y - k)^2 = r^2$ ➔

    c) Plug in the (h, k) = (-4, 1) and

        r = 3/2: $(x - (-4))^2 + (y - (1))^2 = \left(\frac{3}{2}\right)^2$ ➔ $(x + 4)^2 + (y - 1)^2 = \frac{9}{4}$

<u>The Reciprocal Function</u> $y = \dfrac{1}{x}$

- This function can be drawn by plotting points, but before that, there are two asymptotes to discuss.

- The function $y = \dfrac{1}{x}$ has a **horizontal asymptote at y = 0**, which means that the graph gets very close to this line on the y-axis but the graph never crosses or touches the line.

- The function $y = \dfrac{1}{x}$ has a **vertical asymptote** at **x = 0**, which means that the graph gets very close but doesn't touch this vertical line on the x-axis.

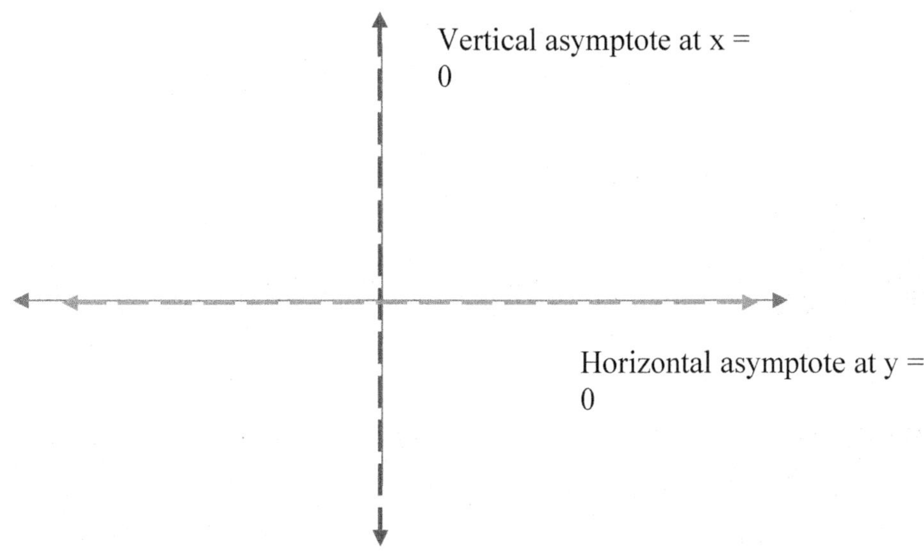

- Now, to understand the graph, plot a few points to the right and to the left of the x = 0 line.

X	$y = \dfrac{1}{x}$
1	$y = \dfrac{1}{(1)} = 1$
-1	$y = \dfrac{1}{(-1)} = -1$
2	$y = \dfrac{1}{(2)} = 0.5$
-2	$y = \dfrac{1}{(-2)} = -0.5$

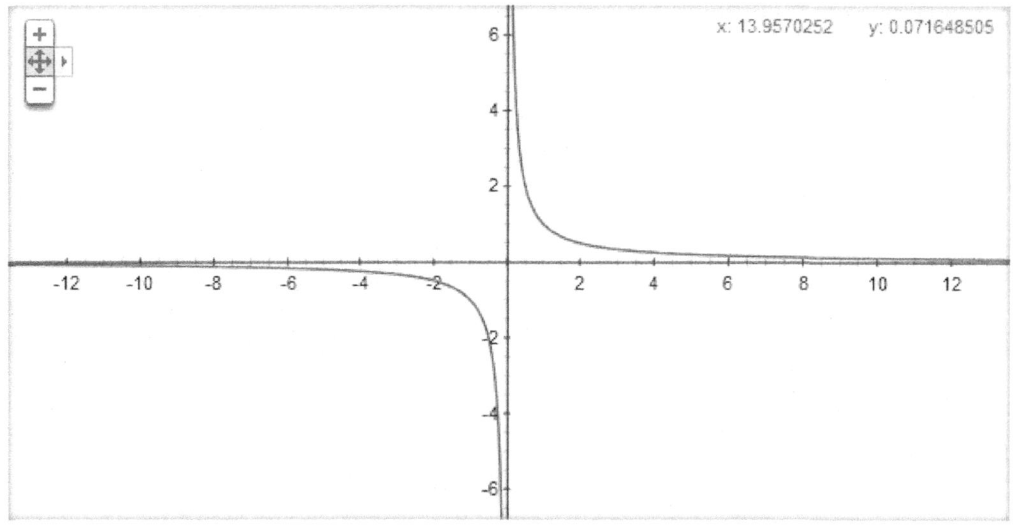

<u>Transforming the Reciprocal Graph</u>

- To move the graph $f(x) = \frac{1}{x}$ up c units, $g(x) = f(x) + c = \frac{1}{x} + c$
- To move the graph $f(x) = \frac{1}{x}$ down c units, $g(x) = f(x) - c = \frac{1}{x} - c$
- To move the graph $f(x) = \frac{1}{x}$ right c units, $g(x) = f(x - c) = \frac{1}{x-c}$
- To move the graph $f(x) = \frac{1}{x}$ left c units, $g(x) = f(x + c) = \frac{1}{x+c}$

Note: For the right and left shifting, the sign is opposite what you would expect! That is not a mistake. It is actually the opposite!

- To **reflect the graph** $f(x) = \frac{1}{x}$ **over the x-axis**, $g(x) = -f(x) = -\frac{1}{x}$.
- To **reflect the graph** $f(x) = \frac{1}{x}$ **over the y-axis**, $g(x) = f(-x) = \frac{1}{-x}$

(You can see that the two reflections will give the same result! This is because of the symmetry already of the parent graph! It has origin symmetry.)

Order of Graphing: Order doesn't matter too much, but it's best to do any reflections first before any shifting right, left, up or down.

Example 6: Identify and label the basic function and then all transformations for $f(x) = -\frac{1}{x-3} + 4$. Label all asymptotes.

Example 7: Graph the functions $f(x) = 2^x$ and $f(x) = \left(\frac{1}{3}\right)^x$.

Solution:

To graph $f(x) = 2^x$, draw in a horizontal asymptote at y =0 since every exponential function starts with the same horizontal asymptote. Then, plot a few points to get the basic shape.

x	$f(x) = 2^x$
0	$f(x) = 2^{(0)} = 1$
1	$f(x) = 2^{(1)} = 2$
2	$f(x) = 2^{(2)} = 4$
-1	$f(x) = 2^{-1} = 1/2$
-2	$f(x) = 2^{-2} = 1/4$

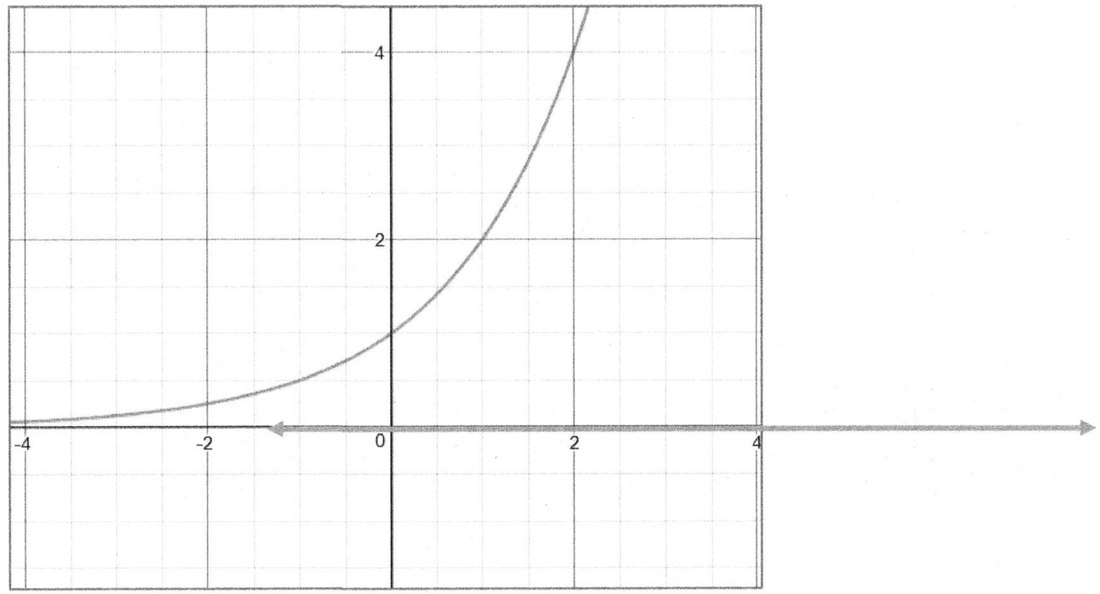

To graph $f(x) = \left(\frac{1}{3}\right)^x$, draw your horizontal asymptote at y = 0 and then plot a few points.

x	$f(x) = \dfrac{1}{3}^x$
0	$f(x) = \dfrac{1^{(0)}}{3} = 1$
1	$f(x) = \dfrac{1^{(1)}}{3} = \dfrac{1}{3}$
2	$f(x) = \dfrac{1^{(2)}}{3} = \dfrac{1}{9}$
-1	$f(x) = \dfrac{1^{(-1)}}{3} = 3$
-2	$f(x) = \dfrac{1^{(-2)}}{3} = 9$

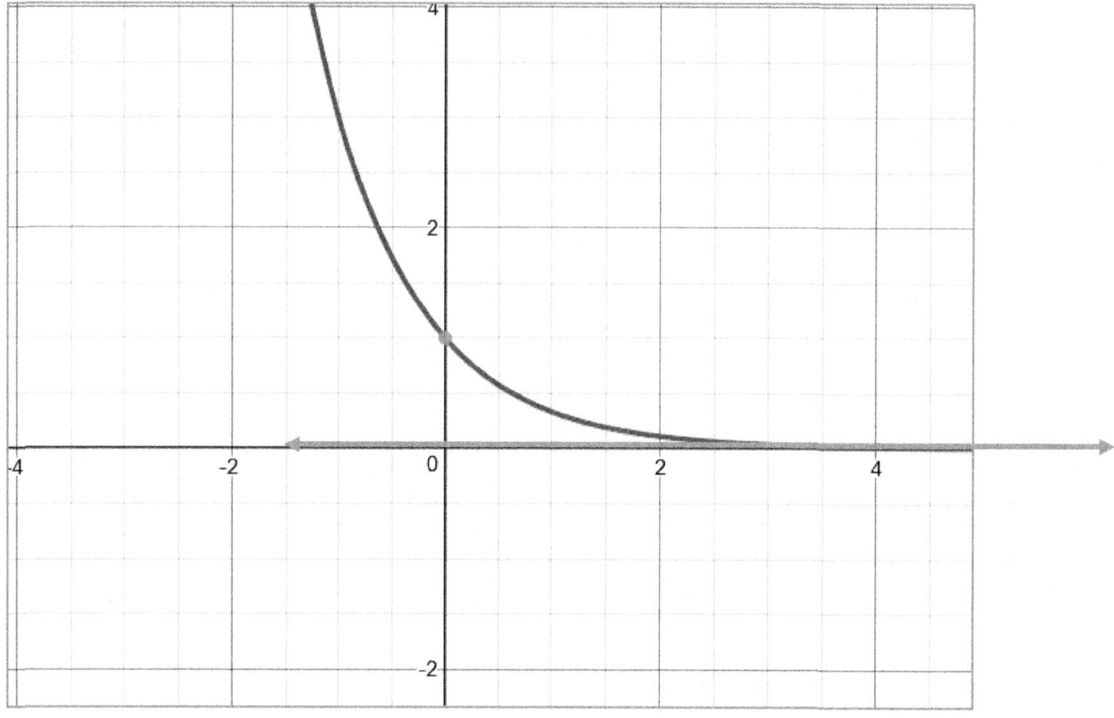

<u>Transformations of $f(x) = b^x$</u>

- To move the graph $f(x) = b^x$ **up c units,** $g(x) = f(x) + c = b^x + c$
- To move the graph $f(x) = b^x$ **down c units,** $g(x) = f(x) - c = b^x - c$
- To move the graph $f(x) = b^x$ **right c units,** $g(x) = f(x - c) = b^{x-c}$
- To move the graph $f(x) = b^x$ **left c units,** $g(x) = f(x + c) = b^{x+c}$

Note: For the right and left shifting, the sign is opposite what you would expect! That is not a mistake. It is actually the opposite!

- To **reflect the graph $f(x) = x^2$ over the x-axis,** $g(x) = -f(x) = -b^x$
- To **reflect the graph $f(x) = x^2$ over the y-axis,** $g(x) = f(-x) = b^{-x}$

The horizontal asymptote starts at y = 0, but **if you move up c units, the HA will become y = c.** Also, **if you move down c units, the HA will become y = c.**

Example 7: For the function $f(x) = -3^{-x} + 1$, find the basic function, graph and label it. Then, graph and label each transformation. Make sure to move the asymptote. Label the new asymptote.

Solution: The basic function is $y = 3^x$, which is exponential growth and has a horizontal asymptote of y = 0.

There is a reflection on the x-axis – from the negative in front of the 3 – and there is also a reflection on the y-axis – from the negative on the exponent's "x". There is also a shift up 1.

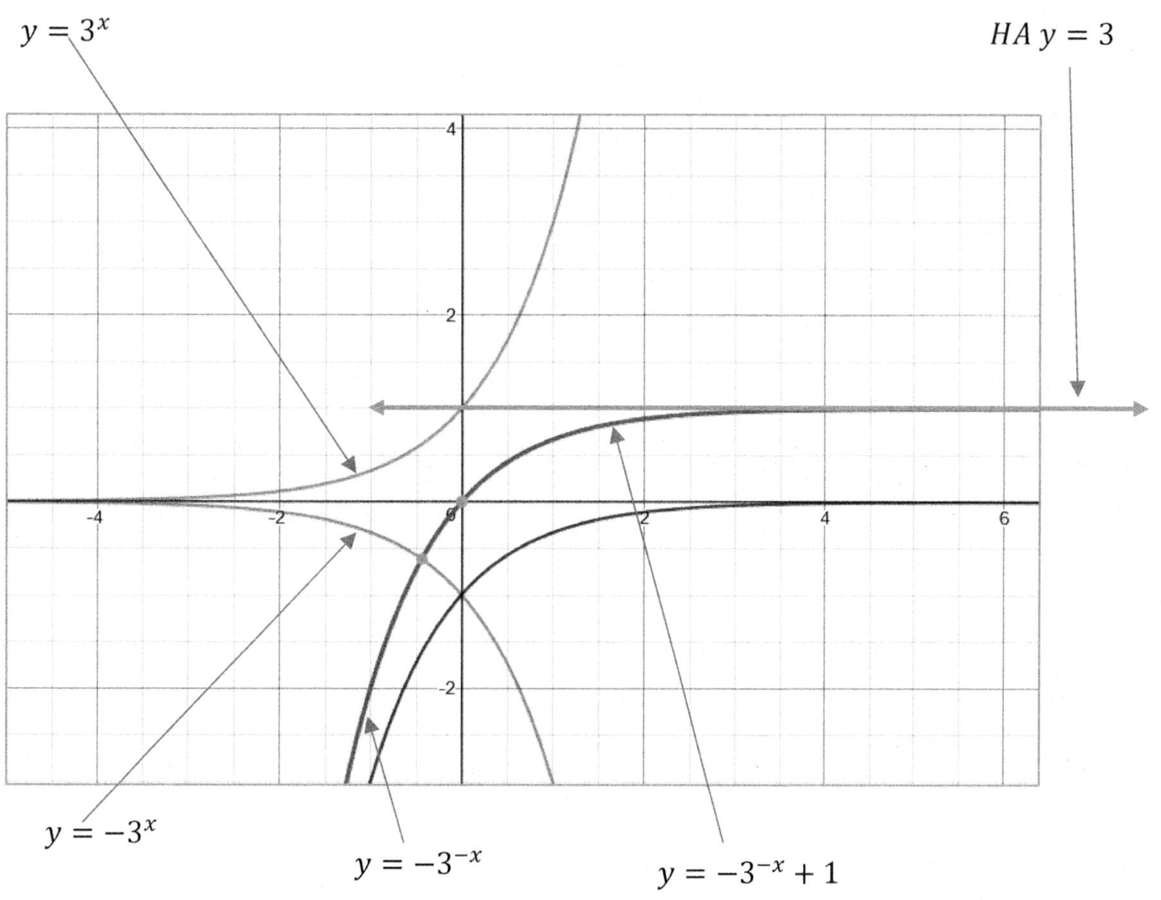

Section 19: Simultaneous Equations

Solving Systems of Linear Equations

To **solve a 2x2 system of linear equations** means find the ordered pair that will make both equations in two variables true at the same time. The variables must be to the first power to be considered linear, and recall that linear means line equations. Therefore, we're solving two line equations at the same time.

Geometrically, it means find all points on both lines, or in the intersection of both lines. There are three possibilities.

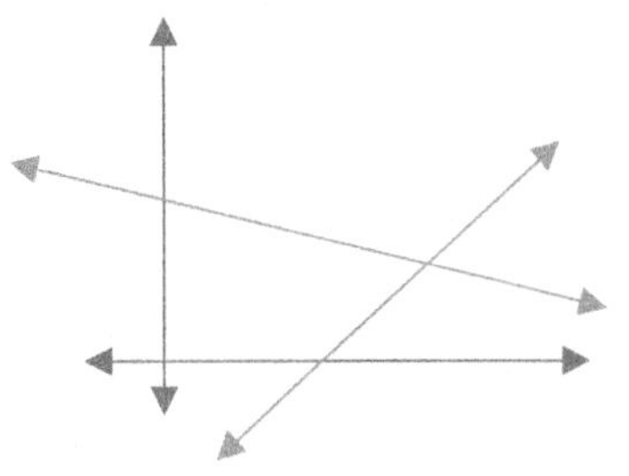 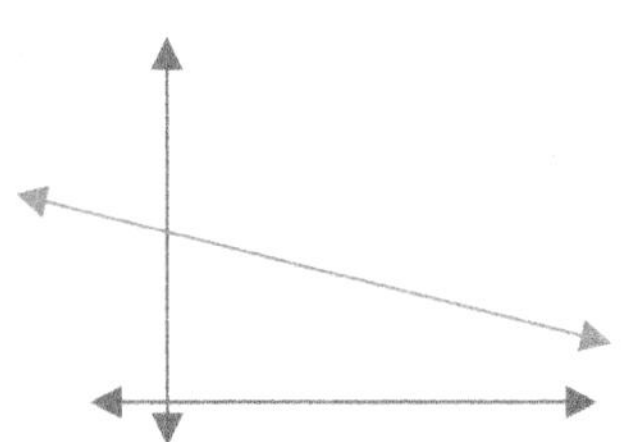 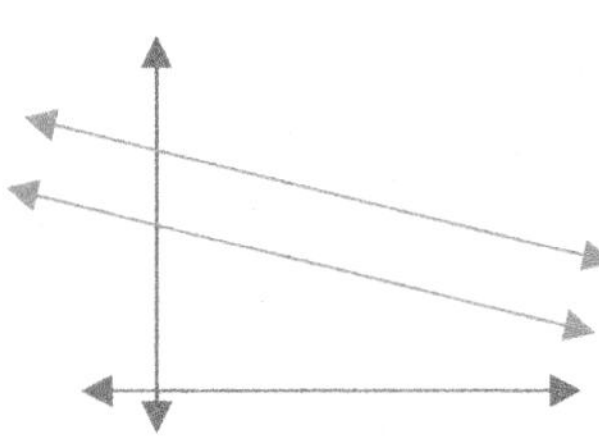

One solution
One point in common
Two intersecting lines

Infinite solutions
All points in common
One line on top of another

No solutions
No points in common
Parallel lines

Method 1: Solve with Substitution – best to do when it is easy to solve for a variable.

Example 1: Solve the system $\begin{cases} 2x - y = 5 \\ y = 5x - 8 \end{cases}$. Check your answer(s).

Solution:

To solve a system, determine the method. Substitution seems like a good method because the second equation is already solved for one variable, namely the "y".

> **Step 1:** Isolate one variable in one equation. $\qquad y = 5x - 8$ (from equation 2)

> **Step 2:** Plug into the same variable y in the first equation. $2x - (5x - 8) = 5$

> Notice in doing so that the "y" is gone and you only have x.

Step 3: Solve for x.

$$2x - (5x - 8) = 5 \rightarrow 2x - 5x + 8 = 5 \rightarrow -3x + 8 = 5 \rightarrow -3x = -3 \rightarrow x = 1$$

Step 4: Now, you need the corresponding y-value. Always go back to either of the original equations, plug in the x-value you found, and find the corresponding y-value. It doesn't matter which equation you use; you'll get the same answer regardless.

Equation 1: $2(1) - y = 5 \rightarrow 2 - y = 5 \rightarrow -y = 3 \rightarrow y = -3$

Recall that the solution of a system is an ordered pair, or a point. It can be written as: $\{(1, -3)\}$, a solution set of an ordered pair.

To check any system, you must plug your values for x and y into both equations to ensure the point is on both lines.

$$2(1) - (-3) = 5 \rightarrow 2 + 3 = 5 \rightarrow 5 = 5$$

$$-3 = 5(1) - 8 \rightarrow -3 = -3$$

Example 2: Solve the system $\begin{cases} 3x = 2y - 7 \\ 2x + 3y = 4 \end{cases}$ by substitution. Check your answer(s).

Solution: To solve this system by substitution, notice it's more difficult because none of the variables are isolated. It doesn't matter which you isolate, but no matter which you choose, there will be fractions.

Step 1: Solve for x in Equation 1. $\qquad 3x = 2y - 7 \rightarrow x = \frac{2y-7}{3}$

Step 2: Plug into x in Equation 2. $\qquad 2x + 3y = 4 \rightarrow 2\left(\frac{2y-7}{3}\right) + 3y = 4$

Step 3: Solve for y. $\qquad \rightarrow \frac{4y-14}{3} + 3y = 4 \rightarrow \left(\frac{4y-14}{3} + 3y\right)(3) = (4)(3)$

$$\rightarrow 4y - 14 + 9y = 12$$

$$\rightarrow 13y = 26 \rightarrow y = 2$$

If you have fractions and are solving an equation, you can simply multiply by the LCD on both sides of an equation and you will cancel all your denominators to 1 and won't have to deal with the fractions anymore! **This will only work with equations though; it will not work with expressions.**

Step 4: Plug y = 2 into either original equation and solve for x.

$$\text{Equation 2: } 2x + 3(2) = 4 \rightarrow 2x + 6 = 4 \rightarrow 2x = -2 \rightarrow x = -1$$

The solution of the system is: $\{(-1, 2)\}$

Check: $3(-1) = 2(2) - 7 \rightarrow -3 = 4 - 7 \rightarrow -3 = -3$

$$2(-1) + 3(2) = 4 \rightarrow -2 + 6 = 4 \rightarrow 4 = 4$$

Method 2: Solve with Addition / Elimination – best to do when it is not easy to solve for a variable. In this method, you want to line up your coefficients on each variable and then multiply one or both equations to make the coefficients the opposite of each other. That way, when you add the equations, the variables will eliminate from the system.

Example 3: Solve $\begin{cases} 2x = 3y + 8 \\ 2y = 4x - 16 \end{cases}$ by elimination. Check your answer(s).

Solution: Notice that none of the variables are isolated. This would be more difficult to do with substitution. With elimination, you should always align the variables, generally on the left side with the constant on the right.

Step 1: Write your system in standard form, with the variables in alphabetical order on the left and the constants on the right of the equal sign.

$$\begin{cases} 2x - 3y = 8 \\ -4x + 2y = -16 \end{cases}$$

Step 2: Examine the coefficients of the variables. You want to be able to make your coefficients the opposite number of each other. If you multiply the first equation by a 2, the coefficient on x will be a 4, and the coefficient on the other equation's x is a -4, which works perfectly. When you add the equations, you'll get 0x, which is what you want.

$$\begin{cases} (2x - 3y = 8)2 \\ -4x + 2y = -16 \end{cases} \rightarrow \begin{cases} 4x - 6y = 16 \\ -4x + 2y = -16 \end{cases}$$

You could multiply both equations by various numbers (positive or negative 3 and 2) to eliminate the y's – there's nothing wrong with this – but it takes more steps and therefore has more chance to make an error.

Step 3: Add up the equations. Then solve for the variable you have left.

-4y = 0 ➔ y = 0

Step 4: Now, just like with substitution, go back to the original system with whatever value you have, plug it into either equation and solve for the variable you don't have.

Equation 1: $2x - 3y = 8$ ➔ $2x - 3(0) = 8$ ➔ x = 4

The solution for the system is: {(4,0)}.

Check: $2(4) = 3(0) + 8$ ➔ $8 = 8$

$2(0) = 4(4) - 16$ ➔ $0 = 16 - 16$ ➔ $0 = 0$

Example 4: Fred bought three hammers and four boxes of screws and he spent $18. Sally spent $7 for two hammers and one box of screws. What is the cost of the hammer and box of screws, assuming they bought the same ones? Set up a system and solve with elimination.

Solution: The unknown quantities are the hammer and the box of screws costs. Let x = the cost of the hammer and y = the cost of the box of screws.

Fred bought three hammers. Each hammer costs $x. He spent $3x on hammers.

Fred also bought four boxes of screws. Each box costs $y. He spent $4y on screws.

In total, Fred spent $3x + $4y = $18. You can drop the dollar signs if you want for neatness.

Sally's equation can be expressed as: 2x + y = 7.

The system would be: $\begin{cases} 3x + 4y = 18 \\ 2x + y = 7 \end{cases}$.

You can solve either way, but to solve with elimination, it would be easy to do so by multiplying Equation 2 by -4 to eliminate the "y" variable.

$$\begin{cases} 3x + 4y = 18 \\ (2x + y = 7)(-4) \end{cases} \rightarrow \begin{cases} 3x + 4y = 18 \\ -8x - 4y = -28 \end{cases} \rightarrow -5x = -10 \rightarrow x = 2$$

Solve for y in Equation 1: 3x + 4y = 18 → 3(2) + 4y = 18 → 4y = 12 → y = 3

The solution that the hammers cost $2 and the box of screws cost $3.

Solving Systems of Non-Linear Equations

When you want to find the intersection of two graphs that are not straight lines, you can solve a system of non-linear equations. One of the graphs could be a straight line, but so long as one graph is not, it is considered a non-linear system.

Example 5: Find where the graphs of $y = \sqrt{x - 3}$ and $y = x - 3$ intersect.

Solution: Although this doesn't look like it, it is a system of equations. The square root equation is not linear because of the square root, so although the second equation is, the system is considered non-linear. To solve, you want to use substitution. You cannot use elimination with non-linear systems except if all the variables are exactly to the same power, and that's not the case in this problem.

Using substitution, set the y in the first equation equal to the y in the second equation:

$$y = y \rightarrow \sqrt{x - 3} = x - 3$$

To solve, square both sides, making sure to distribute through FOIL on the right:

$$\left(\sqrt{x - 3}\right)^2 = (x - 3)^2 \rightarrow x - 3 = x^2 - 6x + 9$$

Now, solve the quadratic.

$$x - 3 = x^2 - 6x + 9 \rightarrow 0 = x^2 - 7x + 12 \rightarrow 0 = (x - 4)(x - 3) \rightarrow x = 4$$

or x = 3

With non-linear systems, it is possible to get more than one solution! It is possible with linear also if the two lines are on top of each other. In this problem, we have two x-values. We have to now go and find the corresponding y-values.

Using Equation 2: $y = x - 3 \rightarrow$ and $y = (4) - 3 = 1 \rightarrow$ (4, 1) is a solution.

$$y = x - 3 \rightarrow \text{ and } y = (3) - 3 = 0 \rightarrow (3, 0) \text{ is a solution.}$$

The solution for this system is: $\{(4,1), (3,0)\}$

If you plot the points, you can see you have the following graphs:

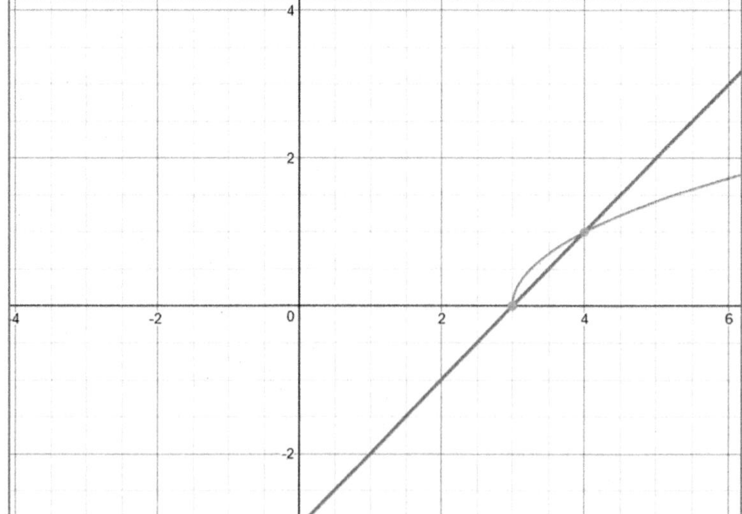

Check:

To check, each point must be plugged into each equation.

(4, 1):

$(0) = \sqrt{4-3}$ ➜ $1 = 1$

$(0) = (4) - (3)$ ➜ $1 = 1$

(3, 0):

$(0) = \sqrt{(3) - 3}$ ➜ $0 = 0$

$(0) = (3) - 3$ ➜ $0 = 0$

Paper 1

Answer ALL NINETEEN questions.
Write your answers in the spaces provided.
You must write down all stages in your working.
You must NOT use a calculator

1. (a) Which digit is in the thousandths place in the number: 1,234.567?

....

[1 mark]

    (b) Convert the improper fraction $\dfrac{17}{6}$ to a mixed number.

....

[2 marks]

    (c) Which of these numbers is largest?

        345   -17   42 3^4

....

[1 mark]
(Total 4 marks)

2. (a) Calculate the value of this expression: $2 + 6 * 3 * (3 * 4)^2 + 1$

. . . .
[2 marks]

(b) Solve for x : $x = \dfrac{3}{4} \times \dfrac{7}{8}$

. . . .
[1 mark]

(c) Solve this equation: $x = 8 - (-3)$

. . . .
[1 mark]

(d) Find the median in this series of numbers: 80, 78, 73, 69, 100

. . . .
[2 marks]
(Total 6 marks)

3. Amy drives her car until the gas gauge is down to 1/8 full, then she fills the tank to capacity by adding 14 gallons.

(a) What is the capacity of the gas tank?

....

[3 marks]

Danvers is 8 miles due south of Carson and 6 miles due west of Baines. If Amy could drive in a straight line from Carson to Baines.

(b) how long would the trip be?

....

[3 marks]
(Total 6 marks)

4.

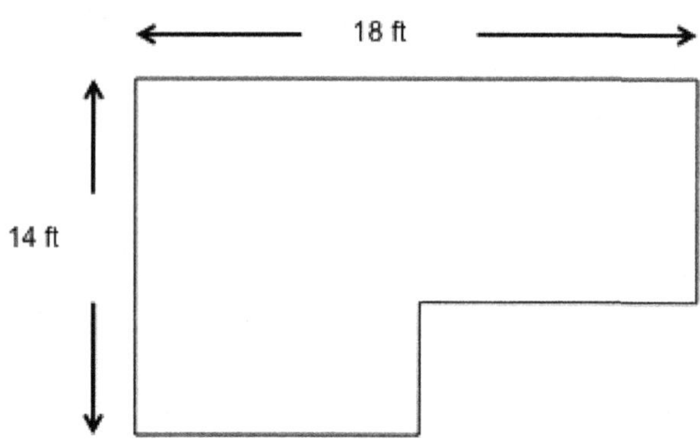

(a) What is the perimeter of the above figure?

. . . .

[2 marks]

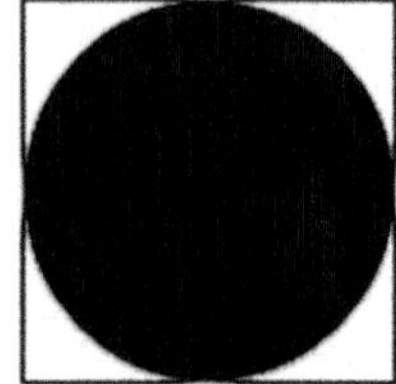

(b) If the radius of the circle in this diagram is 4 inches, what is the perimeter of the square?

. . . .

[2 marks]
(Total 4 marks)

5. Factorize 24 into prime numbers.

. . . .
[2 marks]
(Total 2 marks)

6. Here is a two stage number machine.

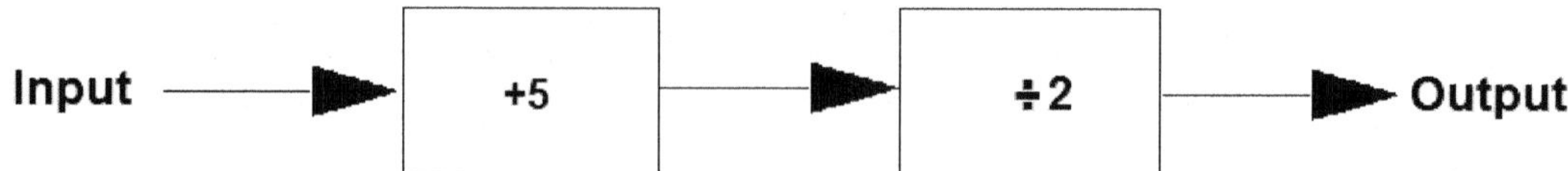

The machine adds 5 and then divides by 2.

(a) What will be the output if input is 5?

....

[2 marks]

Input	Output
0	7
3	13
5	17
7	21
8	23

(b) Fill the number machine for the above table in figure below.

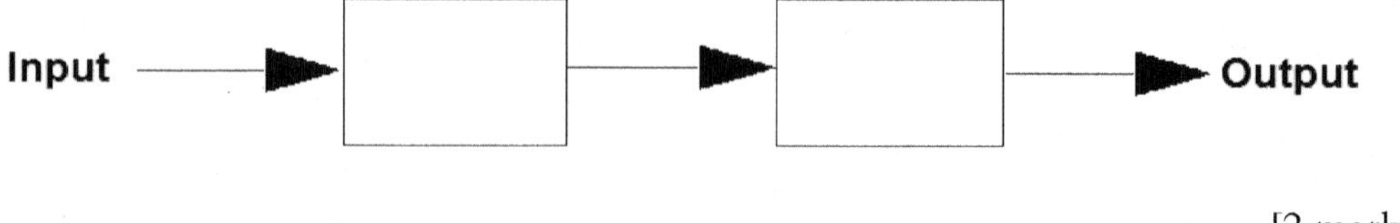

[2 marks]
(Total 4 marks)

7. Jean buys a textbook, a flash drive, a printer cartridge, and a ream of paper. The flash drive costs three times as much as the ream of paper. The textbook costs three times as much as the flash drive. The printer cartridge costs twice as much as the textbook. The ream of paper costs $10. How much does Jean spend altogether?

....
[3 marks]
(Total 3 marks)

8. Brian pays 15% of his gross salary in taxes. He pays $7,800 in taxes.
What is his gross salary?

....
[2 marks]
(Total 2 marks)

9. The ratio of female to male nurses in a hospital is 9:1.
(a) If there are 144 female nurses, how many male nurses are there?

....
[2 marks]

There are 3 more men than women on the board of directors of a hospital There are 13
members on the board.
(b) How many are women?

....
[3 marks]
(Total 5 marks)

10. On a roulette wheel, there are 37 pockets numbered 0 through 36.

   (a) On any given spin, what is the probability that the ball will land on an odd number?

. . . .
[2 marks]

Mark will randomly choose 2 different letters from the word MINUTE.

   (b) If the first letter he chooses is an M or an N, what is the probability that the next letter he chooses will be an M or an N?

. . . .
[2 marks]
(Total 4 marks)

11.

$$-9 \times -9 =$$

(a) Solve this equation

....
[1 mark]

Seven added to four-fifths of a number equals fifteen.

(b) What is the number?

....
[2 marks]

$$x^2 \times x^3$$

(c) Solve this equation

....
[1 mark]
(Total 4 marks)

12. If the sum of two numbers is 360, and their ratio is 7:3.

    (a) what is the smaller number?

....

[2 marks]

    (b) Which is the larger number among $\frac{5}{8}$ *and* 0.72?

....

[1 mark]

Carmen has a box that is 10 inches long, 5 inches wide, and 7 inches high.

    (c) What is the volume of the box?

....

[1 mark]

(Total 4 marks)

13. Alicia must have a score of 75% to pass a test of 80 questions.
    (a) What is the greatest number of questions she can miss and still pass the test?

....
[3 marks]

A cell phone on sale at 30% off costs $210.
(b) What was the original price of the phone?

....
[2 marks]
(Total 5 marks)

14.

$$4,\ 5,\ 4,\ 8,\ 10,\ 4,\ 6,\ 7$$

(a) What is the mode in this set of numbers?

....
[1 marks]

It took Charles four days to write a history paper. He wrote 5 pages on the first day, 4 pages on the second day, and 8 pages on the third day. If Charles ended up writing an average of 7 pages per day.
(b) How many pages did he write on the fourth day?

....
[2 marks]
(Total 3 marks)

15. In the graduating class at Emerson High School, 52% of the students are girls and 48% are boys. There are 350 students in the class. Among the girls, 98 plan to go to college.

How many girls do not plan to go to college?

. . . .

[3 marks]
(Total 3 marks)

16.

(a) Which of the following numbers is a perfect square?

5　　　　15　　　　49　　　　50

....
[1 mark]

(b) Circle the correct statement?

The square of a number is always less than the number.

The square of a number may be either positive or negative

The square of a number is always a positive number.

The square of a number is always greater than the number

[1 mark]

(c) Which of the following is equal to half a billion?

50,000,000　500,000,000　　　　500,000　　　　50,000,000,000

....
[1 mark]
(Total 3 marks)

17. The population of Mariposa County in 2015 was 90% of its population in 2010. The population in 2010 was 145,000.

(a) What was the population in 2015?

....
[2 mark]

Marisol's score on a standardized test was ranked in the 80th percentile. Suppose that 660 students took the exam.

(b) How many students scored lower than Marisol?

....
[2 marks]

In a high school French class, 45% of the students are sophomores, and there are 9 sophomores in the class.

(c) How many students are there in the class?

....
[2 marks]

(Total 6 marks)

18. Amanda makes $14 an hour as a bank teller, and Oscar makes $24 an hour as an auto
mechanic. Both work eight hours a day, five days a week.
(a) How much they make together in a five-day week?

....
[3 marks]

If Amanda worked 40 hours at d dollars per hour and received a bonus of $50, her total
earnings were $530.
(b) What was her hourly wage?

....
[3 marks]

(c) Solve for r in this equation: p = 2r + 3

....
[2 marks]
(Total 8 marks)

19. When you add two numbers, the sum is 480. If the ratio of the two numbers is 5:1.
(a) What is the smaller number?

....
[2 marks]

Two rectangles are proportional; that is, the ratio of length to width is the same for both rectangles. The smaller rectangle has a length of 8 inches and a width of 3 inches. The larger rectangle has a length of 12 inches.
(b) What is the width of the larger rectangle?

....
[2 marks]
(Total 4 marks)

Paper 1 – Answers and Marks

Question	Answer	Marks	Comment
1(a)	10	**B1**	1 is in the thousands place. 2 is in the hundreds place. 3 is in the tens place. 4 is in the ones place 5 is in the tenths place. 6 is in the hundredths place. 7 is in the thousandths place
1(b)	17/6 2 Quotient 5 Remainder	**M1**	
	$2\dfrac{5}{6}$	**B1**	
1(c)	345	**B1**	
2(a)	Multiply the numbers in **Parentheses**: $3 \bullet 4 = 12$ Apply the **Exponent** 2 to the number in parentheses: $12^2 = 144$ **Multiply**: $6 \bullet 3 \bullet 144 = 2{,}592$ **Add**: $2 + 2{,}592 + 1 = 2{,}595$	**M1**	**Parentheses**: The first step is to do any operations in parentheses. **Exponents**: Then do any steps that involve exponents **Multiply** and **Divide**: Multiply and divide from left to right **Add** and **Subtract**: Add and subtract from left to right
	2595	**B1**	
2(b)	$\dfrac{21}{32}$ o.e.	**B1**	
2(c)	11	**B1**	

2(d)	69,73,78,80,100 Median=78	M1	Arrange the given numbers in either ascending or descending order. The middle value after arrangement is the median.
	78	A1	

3	Identify that $\frac{7}{8}$ of the tank is empty or is $\frac{1}{8}$ full	M1	
	Use of ratio to determine the tank's capacity or draw a diagram to represent tank	M1	
	16	A1	

3(b)	Identify the right angle triangle formed by the path followed by driver.	M1	
	$8^2 + 6^2 = c^2$	M1	Apply Pythagoras theorem $\text{hypotenuse}^2 = \text{base}^2 + \text{height}^2$
	10	A1	

4(a)	Identify that right side = left side and top side = bottom side	M1	Perimeter of a shape is the sum of the lengths of all sides.

	64	**A1**	

4(b)	Side of square = 8 Perimeter = 8*4 or 8+8+8+8 = 36	**M1**	Perimeter of a shape is the sum of the lengths of all sides.
	36	**A1**	

5	Write a multiplication fact of 24 e.g. 24 = 6 x 4. Then prime factorize 6 and 4	**M0**	
	24 = 2 x 2 x 2 x 2	**B2**	

6(a)	5 + 5 = 10 10 ÷ 2 = 5	**M1**	
	5	**A1**	

6(b)	x 2	**B1**	
	+ 7	**B1**	

7	Identify that cost of all items can be expressed in terms of cost of ream of paper Develop equation $$x + 3x + 9x + 18x = 31x$$ $$x = 10$$	**M1**	Cost of ream $= x$ Cost of flash drive $= 3x$ Cost of textbook $= 9x$ Cost of printer cartridge $= 18x$
	Total cost $= 31x = 310$	**M1**	
	310	**A1**	

8	$$x \times \frac{15}{100} = 7800$$ $$x = 52000$$	**M1**	
	$52000	**A1**	

9(a)	144/9	**M1**	Identify that the number of male nurses is 9 times less than female nurses.
	16	**B1**	Calculate the exact number of male nurses.

9(b)	$x + (x + 3) = 13$	**M1**	Develop an equation to represent the number of women on the board.
	$2x + 3 = 13$ $2x = 10$	**M1**	Simplify the equation.
	$x = 5$	**A1**	Calculate the number of women.
	Additional Guidance		
	Accept any correct equation developed by the student.		

10(a)	18 odd numbers and 19 even numbers between 0 and 36.	**M1**	Identity correct odd numbers between 0 and 36.
	18/37	**A1**	$\dfrac{\text{Number of odd numbers}}{\text{Number of total numbers}}$

10(b)	Total remaining letters = 5	**M1**	Identify that after the first letter, there will be five letters remaining.
	1/5	**A1**	Calculate the probability of the second letter.

11(a)	81		B1	Negative into negative makes positive

11(b)	$$7 + \dfrac{4x}{5} = 15$$ $$x = 10$$		M1	Write in form of equation
	10		B1	

11(c)	x^5		B1	Exponents are added when bases are multiplied

12 (a)	$\dfrac{3}{10} \times 360$	M1	Identify that the smaller number is $\dfrac{3}{10}$ of 360
	108	B1	

Additional Guidance		
Answer is also to be considered correct if solved using equations		

12(b)	0.72	B1	

12(c)	350	B1	Volume of box equals: height $\times$ width $\times$ length

13 (a)	0.75×80	M1	Identify that 75% of 80 is 60
	$80 - 60$	M1	Subtract 60 from 80 to get maximum number of questions Alicia can miss
	20	B1	

Additional Guidance		
The answer can also be calculated by solving for 25% of 80 directly to get the answer		

13(b)	$0.7x = 210$	**M1**	Identify the equation
	300	**B1**	

14(a)	4	**B1**	Mode is the most repeated value

14(b)	$\dfrac{4 + 5 + 8 + x}{4} = 7$	**M1**	Write equation of the given form
	11	**B1**	

<table>
<tr><td></td><td colspan="3" align="center">Additional Guidance</td></tr>
<tr><td></td><td colspan="2">Question can also be solved by finding the total number of pages he wrote and subtracting (5+4+8) from it</td><td></td></tr>
</table>

15	Total girls = 0.52×350	**M1**	Calculate the total number of girls
	Girls going to college = $182 - 98$	**M1**	Calculate the number of girls not planning on going to college
	84	**A1**	

16(a)	49	**B1**	**sqrt** 49 = 7

16(b)	The square of a number is always a positive number.	**B1**	

16(c)	500,000,000	**B1**	

17(a)	$0.9 * 145,500 = x$ $x = 130, 500$	**M1** **A1**	Convert percentage to decimal. And multiply by population in 2010 to get population in 2015.

17(b)	$.80 * 660 = 528$ 528 students	**M1** **A1**	Convert percentage to decimal Multiply by total number

17(c)	$\dfrac{45}{100} * total\ students = 9$ $total\ students = 9 * \dfrac{100}{45}$	**M1**	Identifies 45% of total is 9.
	$Total\ students\ =\ 20$	**A1**	Solves equation to find total number of students

18(a)	Total Wage $= (14 + 24)$ Total hours worked $= 8*5$ Cumulative wage $= 38 *40$	**M1** **M1**	Add Wages of the Two Multiply the wage with no of hours and number of days worked
	1520	**A1**	

18(b)	$530 = 40d +50$	**M1** **M1**	Develop an equation. Simplify Equation
	12	**A1**	Obtain answer.

18(c)	$p - 3 = 2r$ $r = \dfrac{p-3}{2}$	**M1** **A1**	Make 'r' subject Simplify Equation

19(a)	$x + y = 480$ $y = 5x$ $x + 5x = 480$ $6x = 480$	**M1**	Develop equations that show sum of two numbers is 480. And one number is 5 times the other number.
	$x = 80$ $y = 5x = 400$	**A1**	Simplifies the equations and solves for the two numbers

19(b)	Ratio of sides $= \dfrac{length\ of\ rect.2}{length\ of\ rect.1}$ $= \dfrac{12}{8} = 1.5$	**M1**	Develop equations that show sum of two numbers is 480. And one number is 5 times the other number.
	$width\ of\ rectangle\ 2 =$ $ratio * width\ of\ rectangle\ 1$ $= 1.5 * 3 = 4.5\ cm$	**A1**	Simplifies the equations and solves for the two numbers

Paper 2

Answer ALL TWENTY FIVE questions.
Write your answers in the spaces provided.
You must write down all stages in your working.

1.

(a) Which of the following is a prime number?

$$81 \qquad 49 \qquad 59 \qquad 77$$

....
[1 mark]

(b) If $x \geq 9$, which of the following is a possible value of x?

$$2^3 \qquad 9 \qquad \text{-34} \qquad 8.5$$

....
[1 mark]

(c) Which of the following is the smallest possible integer value of x in this equation:

$$x > 3^2 - 4$$

$$3 \qquad 5 \qquad 6 \qquad 7$$

....
[1 mark]

(Total 3 marks)

2. The number of students enrolled at Two Rivers Community College increased from 3,450 in 2010 to 3,864 in 2015. What was the percent increase?

....
[3 marks]

3. Four friends plan to share equally the cost of a retirement gift. If one person drops out of the arrangement, the cost per person for the remaining three would increase by \$12. What is the cost of the gift?

....
[3 marks]

4. The area of a triangle equals one-half the base times the height.
    (a) What is the area of a triangle that has a base of 6 and a height of 9?

. . . .
[2 marks]

The diagram below shows a perfect square inside a circle.

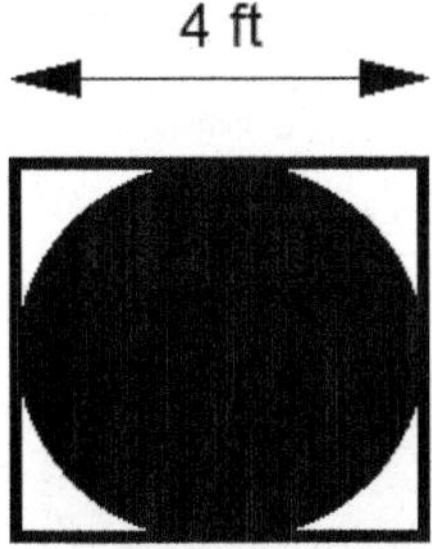

    (b) What is the approximate area of the portion of the square that is not covered by the
         circle?

. . . .
[3 marks]

(Total 5 marks)

5. Simplify the equation

$$\frac{5}{mp} \div \frac{p}{4}$$

....

[2 marks]

6. Lourdes rolls a pair of 6-sided dice. What is the probability that the result will equal 10?

....

[2 marks]

7.

(a) What is the sum of $\frac{1}{8}$ and $\frac{3}{8}$?

....
[1 mark]

(b) What is the least common multiple of 8 and 10?

....
[2 marks]

(c) Solve this equation: $x = -12 \div -3$

....
[1 mark]
(Total 4 marks)

8.

(a) What value of q is a solution to this equation: $130 = q(-13)$

....
[1 mark]

(b) Find the value of $a^2 + 6b$ when $a = 3$ and $b = 0.5$.

....
[2 marks]

(c) What exponent should replace x ?

$$15{,}200 = 1.52 \times 10^x$$

....
[1 mark]

(Total 4 marks)

9. At a lunch cart, there are 2 orders of diet soda for every 5 orders of regular soda. The owner of the lunch cart sells 112 sodas a day.
   (a) How many are diet and how many are regular?

....

[3 marks]

   (b) What is the greatest common factor of 48 and 64?

....

[2 marks]
(Total 5 marks)

10. A rectangle's length is three times its width. The area of the rectangle is 48 square feet.
    (a) How long are the sides?
    Length = 12, width = 4
    Length = 15, width = 5
    Length = 18, width = 6
    Length = 24, width = 8

....

[1 mark]

    (b) x is a positive integer. Dividing x by a positive number less than 1 will yield:

A number greater than x A number less than x
A negative number   An irrational number

....

[1 mark]
(Total 2 marks)

11.

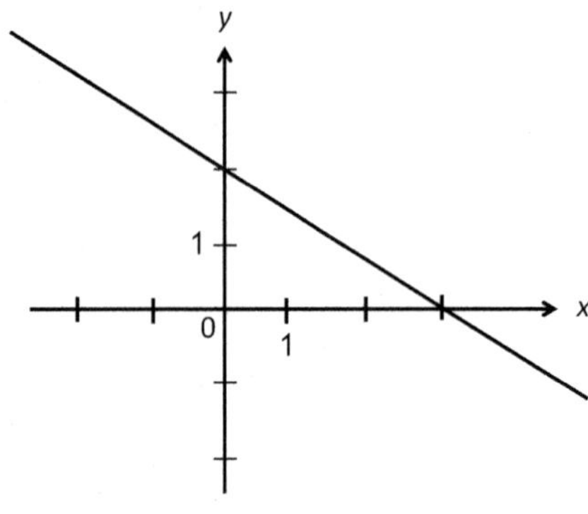

(a) What is the slope of the graph?

. . . .

[2 marks]

(b) What linear equation is depicted in the graph?

. . . .

[2 marks]

(Total 4 marks)

12.

(a) Solve this system of equations:

$$x - 3y = 15$$
$$x + 2y = 25$$

....

[3 marks]

(b) Solve the following equation. Give answer in terms of y.

$$x = y^5 \div y^3$$

....

[2 marks]

(c) Solve this equation:

$$4x^2 + 12x + 5 = 0$$

....

[4 marks]
(Total 9 marks)

13.

    (a) What is the smallest positive integer that is evenly divisible by 5 and 7 and leaves a remainder of 4 when divided by 6?

....

[3 marks]

    (b) What is the sum of all prime numbers less than 25?

....

[2 marks]

(Total 5 marks)

14. Consider a rectangle with a length of 8 and a width of 6. What must be the length of each side of a square that has the same perimeter as the rectangle?

....
[2 marks]

15. Of the patients admitted to an ER over a one-week period, 14 had heart attacks, 15 had workplace injuries, 24 were injured in auto accidents, 12 had respiratory problems, 21 were injured in their homes, and 34 had other medical problems. What percent of these patients had respiratory problems?

....
[3 marks]

16. If $x = -3$ and $y = -5$.

   (a) Find the value of the expression $x^2 + y^3$

[3 marks]

If $a = 10$ and $b = -4$

   (b) What is the value of this expression

$$\sqrt{2a + b^2}$$

[3 marks]

Suppose that $a = -4$

   (c) What is the value of $a^3 - a - 2$?

[3 marks]
(Total 9 marks)

17. The average weight of five friends (Al, Bob, Carl, Dave, and Ed) is 180 pounds. Al weighs 202 pounds, Bob weighs 166 pounds, Carl weighs 190 pounds, and Dave weighs 192 pounds. How much does Ed weigh?

....
[3 marks]

18. Find the number equivalent to 1.34×10^5:

....
[3 marks]

19. The perimeter of a rectangle is 24 inches, and the ratio of the length to the width is 2:1. What is the length and width of the rectangle?

....
[3 marks]

20. Create a stem-and-leaf plot of the data below, which represents the 50-yard freestyle swimming times from yesterday's meet. Use minutes for the stems and seconds for the leaves.

Swimmer	Time
Dawson	24:56
Laraby	24:59
Freemont	24:67
Wallis	24:92
Isles	25:03
Smitherson	25:41
Wilson	25:62
Thomasson	25:63
Billings	25:72
Rawson	25:78
Williams	25:92
Jevers	25:93
Fender	25:94
Marian	26:01
Caldwell	26:32
French	26:73
Icings	26:79
Decker	27:34
Sykes	28:39
Siera	28:47
Penney	29:03

[6 marks]

Paper 2 - Answers and Marks

Question	Answer	Marks	Comment
1(a)	59	**B1**	Chose the correct option
1(b)	9	**B1**	Chose the correct option
1(c)	6	**B1**	Chose the correct option

Question	Answer	Marks	Comment
2	$3864 - 3450 = 414$	**M1**	Find the increase in number of enrollments.
	$\% \ increase = \dfrac{414}{3450} \times 100$ $=12\%$	**M1**	Write the proper equation to calculate the percentage increase
	12%	**A1**	Simplify.

Additional Guidance

Give full marks if direct percentage increase is calculated as follows
$$\left(3864 \times \frac{100}{3450}\right) - 100 = 12\%$$

3	Suppose total cost is $4x$ Thus, $$4x = 3(x + 12)$$	**M1**	Make the correct relationship between total cost of the gift and share of each of the three friends
	$$4x = 3x + 36$$ $$x = 36$$ Total Price $= 4x$ $$= 4 \times 36$$ $$=144$$	**M1**	Solve the equation as follows <ul><li>`Multiply 3 inside the bracket`</li><li>`Subtract 3x from both sides`</li></ul>Total price is $4x$
	$144	**A1**	Calculate the total cost of the gift

<table>
<tr><td colspan="4" align="center">Additional Guidance</td></tr>
<tr><td colspan="3">Give full marks if solved by making following deduction:
When one person dropped out of the arrangement, the cost for the remaining three went up by $12 per person for a total of $36. This means that each person's share was originally $36. Thus, the total cost is $4 \times 36 = \$144$</td><td></td></tr>
</table>

| 4(a) | $$\frac{1}{2} \times 6 \times 9$$
$$= 18$$ | **M1** | Area of a triangle is
$$\frac{1}{2} \times base \times height$$ |
| | 18 | **A1** | Calculate the accurate area |

| 4(b) | Area of square
$$4^2 = 16ft^2$$
radius of circle $= 2ft$
Area of circle
$$3.14 \times 2^2 = 12.56ft^2$$ | **M1** | Area of square $=$ length^2
Identify that radius of the circle is half the length of the square.
Area of circle $= \pi \times radius^2$ |

	Area of the square not covered by the circle $$16 - 12.56 = 3.44 ft^2$$	**M1**	Identify that subtracting the area of circle from the square will give you the area of the portion not covered.
	3.44ft^2	**A1**	Calculate the accurate area

5	$$\frac{5}{mp} \div \frac{p}{4}$$ $$= \frac{5}{mp} \times \frac{4}{p}$$ $$= \frac{20}{mp^2}$$	**M1**	Convert the division sign to multiplication by taking reciprocal and multiply to get the equation simplified
	$$\frac{20}{mp^2}$$	**A1**	Calculate the most simplified form

6	Possible outcomes for the sum to be equal to 10 are (4,6) , (5,5) , (6,4) Total possible outcomes =36 Probability of sum to be 10 $$= \frac{3}{36} = \frac{1}{12}$$	**M1**	Write down the possible values of the two dies at which their sum is 10. There are 3 possible outcomes for such a case. There are 36 total possible outcomes when two dies are rolled. Probability $$= \frac{probable\ outcomes}{total\ possible\ outcomes}$$

	$\dfrac{1}{2}$	**A1**	Calculate the accurate probability

7(a)	$\dfrac{17}{24}$	**B1**	

7(b)	8, 16, 24… 10, 20, 30…	**M1**	Write multiples of 8 and 10
	40	**B1**	Identify the smallest similar number among the multiples

7(c)	4	**B1**	

8(a)	-10	**B1**	

8(b)	$3^2 + 6(0.5)$	**M1**	Substitute values in equation
	12	**B1**	

8(c)	4	**B1**	The decimal moves one place to the left with each increasing power of 10

9(a)	$\dfrac{5}{7} \times 112 = x$ $\dfrac{2}{7} \times 112 = y$	**M1**	Identify the equation
	x = 80, y= 32	**M1**	Calculate no. of regular sodas (x) and diet sodas (y).
	80, 32	**B1**	

9(b)	48 = 1, 2, 3, 4, 6… 64 = 1, 2, 3, 4, 8…	**M1**	Write factors of 48 and 64
	16	**B1**	

| 10(a) | Length = 12, width = 4 | B1 | Length is thrice the width and length into width is 48 |

| 10(b) | A number greater than x | B1 | Dividing x by a positive number less than 1 will yield a number greater than x |

| 11(a) | Slope of the line $= \dfrac{2}{3}$ | M1 | $Slope = \dfrac{rise}{run}.$ |
| | Sign of the slope = negative | M1 | The line is moving downward from left to right |

| 11(b) | Slope of the line = 2/3 | M1 | Slope = rise/run. |
| | Sign of the slope = negative | M1 | The line is moving downward from left to right |

12(a)	$-5y = -10$ or $5x = 105$	**M1**	Eliminate one of the variables.
	y = 2 or x=21	**M1**	Solve for one of the variables.
	x = 21, y= 2	**M1**	Substitute in original equation.

12(b)	$y^{(5-3)}$	**M1**	Identify that the bases are same. Subtract the exponent of the divisor from the exponent of the dividend.
	y^2	**B1**	

12(c)	$ax^2 + bx + c = 0$	M1	Identify that the given function is a quadratic equation.
	$x = \dfrac{-12 \pm \sqrt{12^2 - 4(4)(5)}}{2(4)}$	M1	Input correct values in the quadratic formula.
	$x = \dfrac{-12 \pm \sqrt{64}}{8}$ $x = \dfrac{-12 \pm 8}{8}$ $x = \dfrac{-4}{8}$ or $\dfrac{-20}{8}$	M1	Simplify the equation
	$x = -\dfrac{1}{2}$ or $-2\dfrac{1}{2}$	A1	Calculate the two possible answers.

13(a)	Numbers divisible by both 5 and 7 = 35, 70, 105, 140, 175…	M1	Identify the positive integers divisible by both 5 and 7.
	Multiples of 6 = 6, 12, 18, 24, 30, 36, 42, 48, 54, 60, 66, 72, 78	M1	Identify the positive integers divisible by 6.
	$70 - 66 = 4$ so answer = 70	M1	Choose the correct combination that satisfies given condition.

13(b)	Prime number less than 25 = 2, 3, 5, 7, 11, 13, 17, 19, and 23	**M1**	Identify prime numbers less than 25.
	Sum = 100	**A1**	Calculate the sum of prime numbers.
	Additional Guidance		
	1 is not considered a prime number.		

14	Perimeter = 28	**M1**	Calculate the perimeter of the rectangle.
	Length of each side = 7	**A1**	Identify length of sides from the given perimeter.

15	$14 + 15 + 24 + 12 + 21$ $= 120$	**M1**	Calculate the total number of patients
	$\dfrac{12}{120} \times 100$	**M1**	Calculate the required percentage by dividing the number of patients with respiratory problems by total no. of patients and multiplying with 100.
	10%	**B1**	

16(a)	$(-3)^2 + (-5)^3$	**M1**	Identity the equation by substituting values of x and y.
	$-3 \times -3 = 9$ $-5 \times -5 \times -5 = -125$ $16 + (-125)$	**M1**	Calculate the expression by squaring and cubing values of -3 and -5 respectively
	-116	**B1**	

16(b)	$\sqrt{2(10) + (-4)^2}$	**M1**	Identity the equation by substituting values of x and y.

	$2 \times 10 = 20$ $-4 \times -4 = 16$ $\sqrt{20 + 16}$	**M1**	Calculate the expression by finding square of -4 and product of 2 and 10.
	$\sqrt{36}$	**B1**	

16(c)	$(-4)^3 - (-4) - 2$	**M1**	Identity the equation by substituting value of a.
	$-4 \times -4 \times -4 = -64$ $-(-4) = 4$ $-64 + 4 - 2$	**M1**	Calculate the expression by cubing -4.
	-62	**B1**	

17	$\dfrac{166+190+192+202+Ed}{5} = 180$	**M1**	Identify the average expression.
	$750 + Ed = 5 \times 180$ $Ed = 900 - 750$	**M1**	Calculate Ed's weight.
	150	**B1**	

18	$10^5 = 100000$ $1.34 = 134 \times 10^{-2}$	**M1**	Identify how indices and decimal points work.
	1.34×100000	**M1**	Calculate the expression knowing how decimal point shifts.
	134000	**B1**	

19	$Perimeter = 2(length + width)$ $\dfrac{24}{2} = length + width$	**M1**	Identify the expression using the formula of perimeter
	$Width = \dfrac{length}{2}$ $12 = length + \dfrac{length}{2}$	**M1**	Identify and calculate length and width using given ratios.
	Length = 8, Width = 4	**B1**	

<table>
<tr><td>20</td><td>

Stem	Leaf
24	56 59 67 92
25	41 62 63 72 78 92 93 94
26	01 32 73 79
27	34
28	39 47
29	03

</td><td>A6</td><td>Draw a proper stem and leaf table</td></tr>
</table>

Additional Guidance

Give 1 mark for each correct stem and leaf row

Paper 3

Answer ALL FOURTEEN questions.
Write your answers in the spaces provided.
You must write down all stages in your working.

1.

(a) What is the factorial of 5?

....
[1 mark]

(b) Convert $2\frac{1}{3}$ to an improper fraction.

....
[1 mark]

(c) What is the smallest positive integer that is evenly divisible by 5 and 7 and leaves a remainder of 4 when divided by 6?

35 70 105 140

....
[2 marks]

(Total 4 marks)

2.

(a) What is the value of x in the following equation?

$$\frac{4}{9}x - 3 = 1$$

....

[2 marks]

(b) The product of two numbers is 6 more than their sum. Write equation that describes this relationship?

....

[2 marks]

(c) Alan commutes 18 miles to work. Bob's commute is 4 miles shorter. Ted's commute
is 6 miles shorter than Bob's. Rebecca's commute is shorter than Alan's but longer
than Bob's. What is the length of Rebecca's commute?

....

[3 marks]

(Total 7 marks)

3.

(a) Which of the following is equivalent to 60% of 90?

0.6 x 90   90 ÷ 0.6   3/5   2/3

....

[1 mark]

(b) The perimeter of a rectangle is 24 inches, and the ratio of the length to the width is 2:1. What is the area of the rectangle?

....

[3 marks]

(c) Five students volunteered to paint a room in the community center. If the painters estimated they would finish the job with 2 ½ man-days, how long should it take the students?

....

[3 marks]

(d) At Pleasantville College, the ratio of female to male students is exactly 5 to 4. If the number of students at the college is 3105, how many of them are girls?

....

[3 marks]
(Total 10 marks)

4.

(a) The area of a triangle equals one-half the base times the height. Write the correct way to calculate the area of a triangle that has a base of 6 and a height of 9?

....
[2 marks]

(b) The tree near your house casts a shadow of 27 feet. At the same time of day, your house which is 40 feet tall at the peak of the roof casts a shadow of 68 feet. What must be the tree's height (Give answer in integers)?

....
[4 marks]
(Total 6 marks)

5.

   (a) The lines in the diagram below are

   Parallel   Perpendicular   Acute   Obtuse

....
[1 mark]

   (b) What is the slope of the line in this graph?

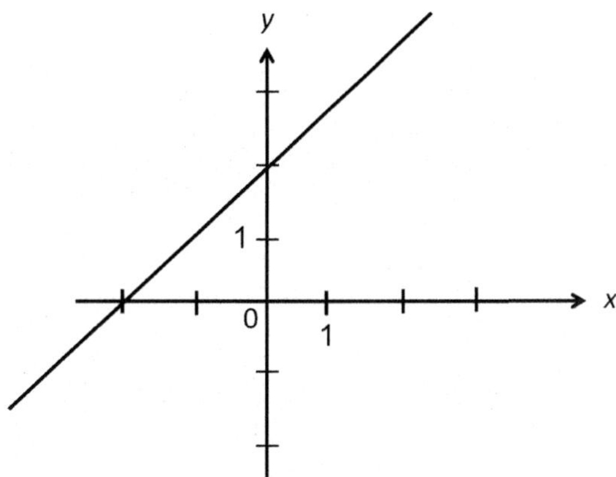

....
[3 marks]

(c) Find linear equation depicted by this graph:

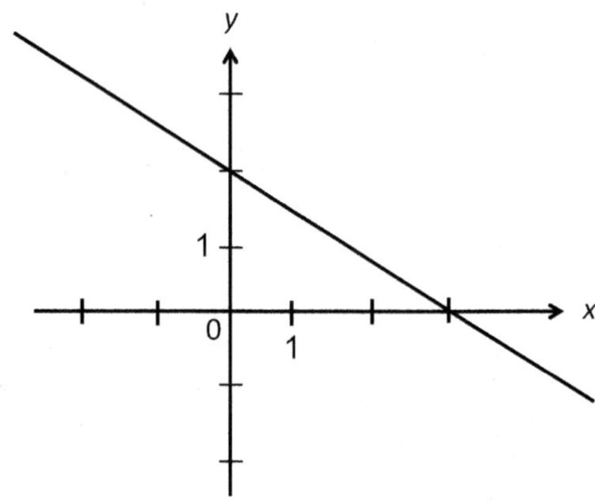

....

[3 marks]

(d) If the y-intercept of the depicted line is reduced by 1, what would be the slope of the
resulting line?

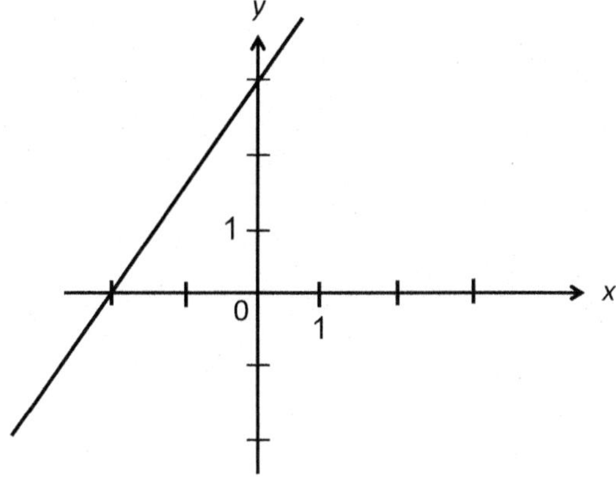

....
[3 marks]
(Total 10 marks)

6.

(a) Which of the following is equivalent to $1.34 * 10^5$?

134,000   13,400   1,340,000   13,400,000

....
[1 mark]

(b) Evaluate Following expression:

$$4^2 \text{ x } 5 \text{ x } 3$$

....
[2 marks]

(c) Evaluate the value of:

$$\frac{3 \times 7^2}{\sqrt[3]{27}}$$

....
[3 marks]
(Total 6 marks)

7.

(a) Solve the inequality $16 - 2x < x$

....

[1 mark]

(b) Given that m is an integer, where $-10 \leq 3m < -3$, find the possible values of m.

....

[2 marks]

(Total 3 marks)

8. The temperatures, in °C, at midnight on 14 consecutive days were

$$-1, \ 0, \ 0, \ 0, \ 1, \ 0, \ -2, \ -1, \ -3, \ 1, \ 2, \ 3, \ 3, \ 2$$

(a) Find the mode of these temperatures.

....

[1 mark]

(b) Find the median of these temperatures.

....

[1 mark]

(c) Find the mean of these temperatures.

. . . .

[1 mark]

(Total 3 marks)

9. The speed of light is given as 3×10^8 m/s

(a) What is the distance, in meters, that light travels in one minute?

. . . .

[2 marks]

(b) What is the time, in seconds, that light takes to travel 100 km?

. . . .

[2 marks]

(Total 4 marks)

10. C is the midpoint of the line joining A and B.

(a) R lies on AB produced, such that $3AR = AB$. Find AC: AR.

....
[2 marks]

(b) If A is $(1, -2)$ and B is $(5, 6)$. Find C.

....
[2 marks]

(c) The line $4x + ky + 10 = 0$ passes through B $(5, 6)$. Find the value of k.

....
[3 marks]

(Total 7 marks)

11. The diagram is the speed-time graph of the last 25 seconds of a car's journey.

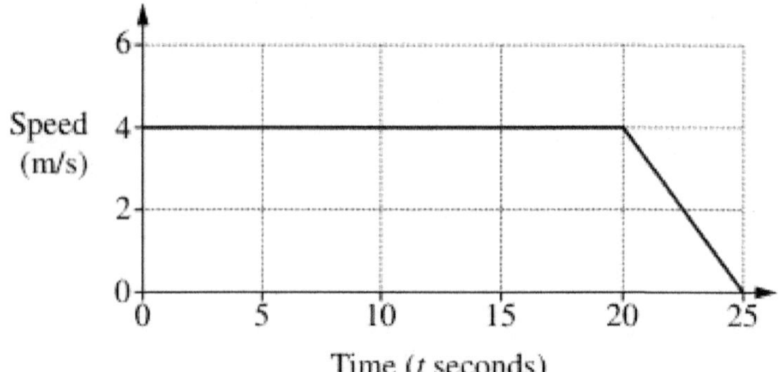

From t = 0 to t = 20 the car moves with a constant speed of 4 m/s.
From t = 20 to t = 25 the car moves with a constant retardation.

(a) What is the acceleration at t= 10 seconds?

....

[1 mark]

(b) Calculate the retardation when t = 22.5.

....

[2 marks]

(c) Show that the distance travelled during the 25 seconds is 90 m.

....

[2 marks]

(d) On the grid below, draw the distance-time graph for the 25 seconds

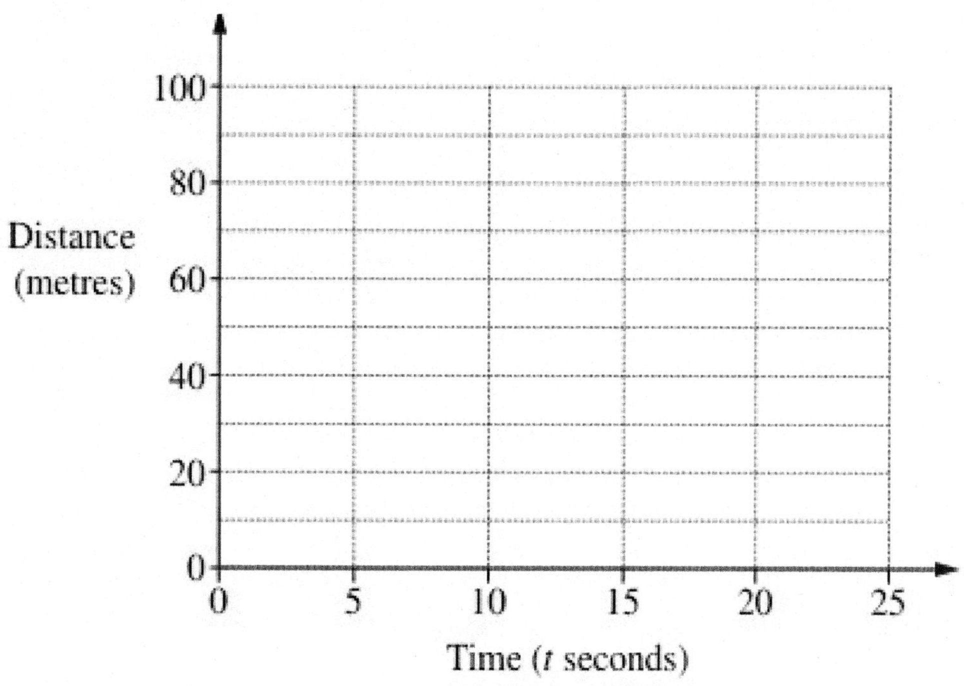

[4 marks]

(Total 9 marks)

12. The radius of the circle, centered O, is 9 cm and the sector angle is 100 degrees.

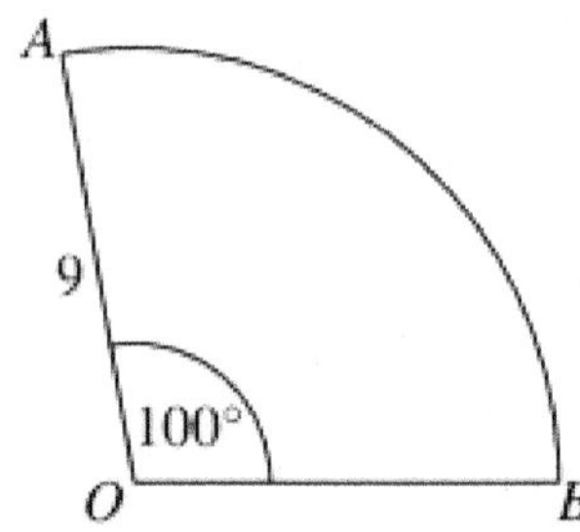

Taking the value of π to be 3.14, calculate

(a) the length of the arc AB,

....
[3 marks]

(b) the perimeter of the sector,

....
[2 marks]
(Total 5 marks)

13. A committee studying an economic issue includes 3 state legislators, 6 state employees, and several members of the public. If one person is selected at random from the committee, the probability that the person will be a state legislator is 1/5.

(a) How many of the members of the committee are members of the public?

....
[1 mark]

(b) What is the probability of the state employees?

....
[1 mark]

(Total 2 marks)

(a) If $a = -4$, what is the value of $a^3 - a - 2$?

....
[2 marks]

(b) The three teams with the best records in the division are the Bulldogs, the Rangers, and the Statesmen. The Bulldogs have won nine games and lost three. The Rangers have won ten games and lost two. The Statesmen have also won ten games and lost two. Each team has one game left before the playoffs. The Bulldogs will be playing the Black Sox, and the Rangers will be playing the Statesmen. The team with the best record will win a spot in the playoffs. Which of the following statements is true?

The Statesmen will definitely be in the playoffs.
The Bulldogs will definitely not be in the playoffs.
The Rangers will definitely not be in the playoffs.
The Statesmen will definitely not be in the playoffs.

[2 marks]

(Total 4 marks)

Paper 3 - Answers and Marks

Question	Answer	Marks	Comment
1(a)	120	**A1**	Evaluate the correct answer 5*4*3*2*1
1(b)	7/3	**A1**	Evaluate the correct answer
1(c)	70	**B2**	Chose the correct option

Question	Answer	Marks	Comment
2(a)	Make x a subject and solve for it	**M1**	Simplify
	9	**A1**	
2(b)	Take two numbers to be unknowns. Identify their product and sum.	**M1**	
	$xy = x + y + 6$	**A1**	It is not necessary the numbers to be x or y.
2(c)	List down commute time of every individual with donating Rebeca's as an unknown (like R)	**M2**	
	14<R<18	**A1**	Candidate can also show range without inequality

Question	Answer	Marks	Comment
3(a)	0.6x90	**B1**	
3(b)	Donate one side as unknown (like width =W) and solve for equation **24=2W+W** Find W and corresponding length	**M2**	

	Length= 2W Find Area **Length * W**		
	128	**A1**	
3(c)	From the information 2.5 man days take to paint one room, then 5 students would provide 5 man days	**M2**	Candidate should mention his reasoning to reach the answer
	½ day	**A1**	
3(d)	Find the fraction 5/9 for girls in school. Multiply it with total number of students.	**M2**	
	1725	**A1**	

4(a)	Identify height and length appropriately.	**M1**	
	½*9*6	**A1**	
4(b)	Identify height of house and its corresponding shadow. Use proportionality to relate height of house with tree.	**M3**	
	16 feet	**A1**	
5(a)	Perpendicular	**B1**	Lines that form a right angle are called perpendicular.
5(b)	Either identify with one step increase in x we get 1 step increase in x or identify points (-2,0) and (0,2) to find slope using slope= (2-0)/(0+2)	**M2**	
	1	**A1**	

5(c)	Find slope using slope = (y2-y1)/(x2-x1) Slope=-2/3	M1	
	Identify y-intercept to be 2	M1	
	y = -2/3x+2	A1	
5(d)	Find slope by identifying points to be (0,2) and (-2,0)	M2	
	1	A1	

6(a)	134,000	B1	
6(b)	240	A2	
6(c)	Simplify to 7^2	M1	
	49	A2	

7(a)	x>16/3	A1	
7(b)	Divide whole inequality by 3	M1	
	-10/3≤m<-1	A1	

8(a)	0	A1	
8(b)	0	A1	

8(c)	0.357	**A1**	5/14 or to two decimal places acceptable

9(a)	Use speed=distance/time	**M1**	
	$1.8 \times 10^{10} m$	**A1**	
9(b)	Use speed= distance/ time	**M1**	
	$3.333 \times 10^{-4} s$	**A1**	

10(a)	Take AC=1/2AB Take AR=1/3 AB	**M1**	
	3/2	**A1**	
10(b)	Use $(\frac{x2+x1}{2}, \frac{y2+y1}{2})$	**M1**	
	C(3,2)	**A1**	
10(c)	Put B(5,6) in equation.		
	K= -5	**A1**	

11(a)	0	**A1**	

11(b)	Realize deceleration is constant and use point at t=20 and t=25 t evaluate it	**M1**	
	-4/5	**A1**	
11(c)	Area under the velocity-time curve is the distance. Area of rectangle =80 Area of triangle= 10 =80+10 90	**M2**	
11(d)	Straight line from 0 to 20 seconds showing constant velocity. Curviness from 20 to 25 seconds.	**M4**	

12(a)	Arc length can be found using proportionality of circumference with 100 degrees' angle. 100/360*2*pi*9	**M2**	

	15.7cm	**A1**	

12(b)	Add arc length and sides of sector	**M1**	
	33.7cm	**A1**	

13(a)	6	**A1**	
13(b)	2/5	**A1**	

14(a)	-62	**A2**	
14(b)	The Bulldogs will definitely not be in the playoffs.	**A2**	The Rangers are playing the Statesmen in the final game, so one of these teams will finish with a record of eleven wins and two losses. Even if the Bulldogs win their game, their final record will be ten wins and three losses. So the Bulldogs will not be in the playoffs.

Printed in Great Britain
by Amazon